HONEY HOLLOW CAMP
BOLTON, VERMONT

EST^D 1941

A PHOTOGRAPHIC HISTORY

JOHN A. WOODEN

FOREWORD BY BRYAN FARNSWORTH

Special Thanks to Edith Wurm Jensen

The majority of the images in this volume were captured by the Wurm and Holmes families from 1940-1965, and are sourced primarily from the photo album of the late Edith Samson Wurm. Her original 35-page book, labeled "Snapshots", has grooved plywood covers stained in dark brown, and heavy black paper pages bound with leather strips. It contains 105 small black and white photos—mostly 3"x2"—affixed to pages with adhesive corners. Scores of these images have been digitally restored, enhanced, and enlarged for this book. Additionally, various color images from 1944-1948 are sourced from single frames captured from Kodak 16mm home movies. All Wurm family imagery appears courtesy of Edith Wurm Jensen.

Thanks also to Bryan Farnsworth, Jennifer Jensen, the Lafreniere Family, Jennifer Wooden Mitchell, Carl Mitchell, Grant Mitchell, Rosemary Wooden Webb, Anne Imhoff, and Carol Devlin of the Bolton Town Clerk Office.

For Martha & Kenneth Wooden

HONEY HOLLOW CAMP
A PHOTOGRAPHIC HISTORY
Copyright ©2021 John A. Wooden

Library of Congress Control Number: 2021903055
ISBN: 978-1-7344706-3-5

By John A. Wooden
www.johnwooden.com

Written & produced under quarantine in Los Angeles, California during the COVID-19 pandemic of 2020-2021.

Photography © Dr. Carl Wurm Jr., Edith Samson Wurm, Ralph Holmes, Mary Holmes, George Samson, Edith Wurm Jensen, John A. Wooden, Kenneth Wooden, the Lafreniere Family, Bryan Farnsworth, Jennifer Wooden Mitchell, Grant Mitchell, Gary Bressor, Burlington Free Press, Vermont Historical Society & Richmond Historical Society.
Dark paper background texture & white-tailed deer photo via Shutterstock.
Color satellite photo via Google Maps. Historical Newspaper Clippings via Newspapers.com and the New York Times.

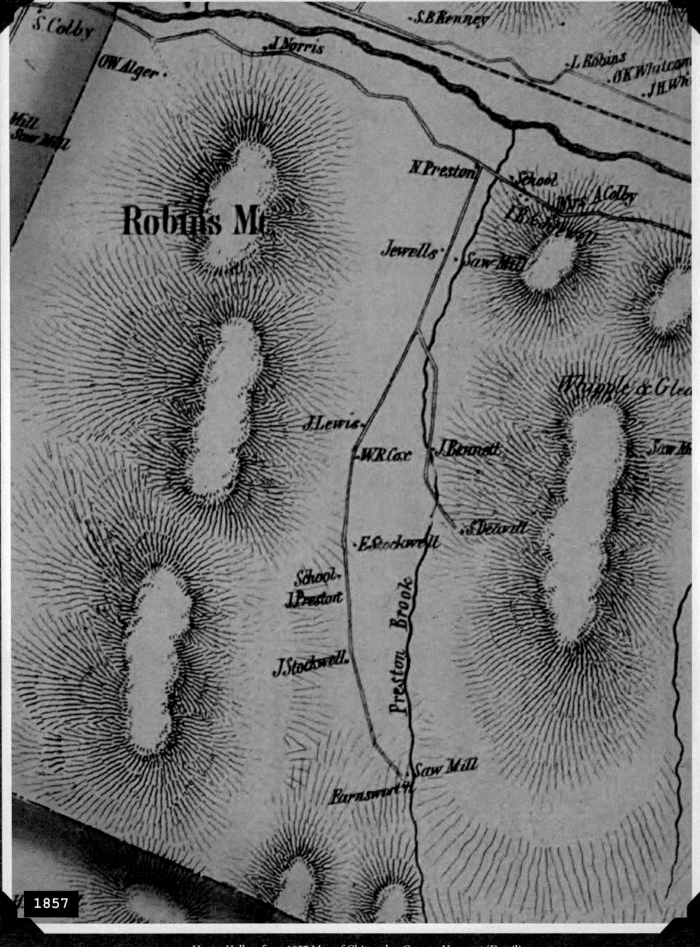

1857

Honey Hollow from 1857 Map of Chittenden County, Vermont (Detail)

6

Honey Hollow as seen looking south across the Winooski River, July 1908.

FOREWORD

As a kid growing up just about a mile away from Honey Hollow in small town Bolton, Vermont, I knew my family had roots along the mountainous back road that runs along Preston Brook. On weekends in the 1990s, my family would ride up into the Hollow to "check things out". Bouncing around in the back of my father's Chevy pickup, it was as if we were security guards for this area of the mountains, keeping an eye on the Wooden and Burns camps, and watching for deer, turkeys and other wildlife often hiding in the thick brush along the road.

Driving through the forest, only long stretches of moss-covered stone walls and a few scattered old apple trees hinted that, in days gone by, people called these woods home. When I was young, I'd heard the stories of my maternal great-grandparents in Honey Hollow: Leo Lafreniere logging and making maple syrup at his sugar house, and later, Judy Preston Lafreniere's dying wish to have the valley preserved as part of Camel's Hump State Forest. But then as I grew older, I discovered that my paternal Farnsworth ancestors once operated a sawmill in Honey Hollow, too—and I was inspired to learn more about the history of this tranquil, secluded place.

In the mid-18th century, the "New Huntington" area was still a wilderness territory. The Onion River (now called the Winooski River) was the primary trade and travel route used by Native Americans and militia during the French and Indian War. The town of Bolton was formally chartered in 1763, but settlement remained sparse; only 88 residents were recorded in the very first census of 1790.

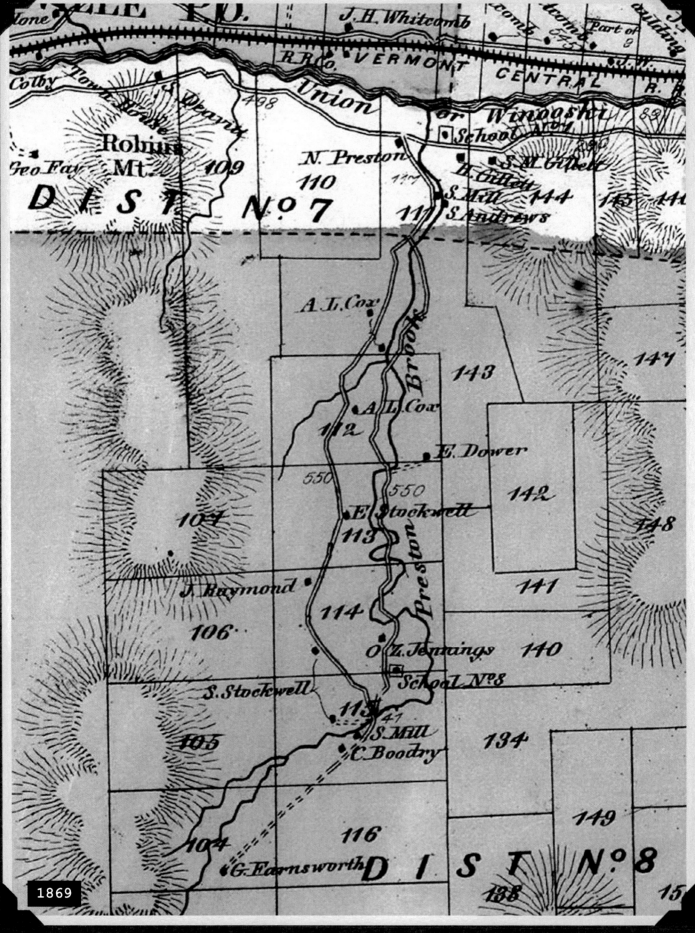

1869

Honey Hollow with two parallel roads, from 1869 map of Bolton VT. (Detail)

In 1792, an intrepid settler named John Preston purchased over 400 acres across Bolton, including a large tract of farm land stretching from the south banks of the Winooski into the lower parts of Honey Hollow. He and his family would settle at the base of a roaring mountain brook that would later bear his name. There they raised cattle, grew vegetables, and made charcoal and potash from the abundant lumber that surrounded them—shipping their goods two miles down the river to Jonesville for trade.

It was along Preston Brook's clear, cold waters flowing from the summit of Camel's Hump that families settled Honey Hollow over the next century. The Jewells made their home just above the Prestons, operating a sawmill. Above them, the Stockwell family cleared large plots including one with sweeping views of Camel's Hump and Bolton Valley, where they built a farm, grew apples and produced maple syrup. Higher still, Francis Farnsworth and family acquired a sawmill and home at the two mile mark where the road crosses the brook.

By the 1840s, over 1000 sawmills were operating across Vermont, and with the completion of the Central Vermont Railroad along the Winooski River, the Honey Hollow region joined the state-wide lumber boom. Additional mills sprung up along Preston Brook's higher elevations, processing soft pine, maple, white birch and other trees into straight board lumber, shingles, and products such as cheese boxes and butter tubs.

By 1857, not one but two roads ascended the valley: the original Honey Hollow Road on the west side of the brook, and a second logging road that crisscrossed Preston Brook seven times before the two roads merged close to the Farnsworth mill. Steps away, a new schoolhouse near the Jennings homestead provided basic education to children from the many families settling along the roads, including the Lewis, Deavitt and Cox clans.

When turmoil between the North and South broke out causing the Civil War, Honey Hollow's Henry and Silas Farnsworth were among the 66 Bolton men who answered the call for the Union. After the war,

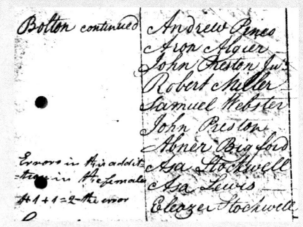

1790 Census: Bolton, Vermont

Photo: The Lafreniere

Third generation Prestons, William & Jessie, c. 1910

Mill up Honey Hollow.

Looking down the Hollow.

July 2, 1893

Photo: Richmond Historical Society

many returned home and acquired new land in Honey Hollow with their war earnings. Another school, the Fiddock School, was built yards from the base of Honey Hollow Road to accommodate the growing population.

For the rest of the 1800s, lumbering and farming was a way of life in Honey Hollow, and property records document its residents' comings and goings. After the Jewetts ventured west to settle in California's post-Gold Rush Sonoma Valley, Samuel Andrews occupied their property. Eleazer Stockwell and his eldest son Sylvester had two large plots, and Joseph Raymond purchased land just north of the big Stockwell farm. The Farnsworth family moved out of Honey Hollow for other lumbering opportunities in Waterbury, except for son George, who settled even further up the mountain, remaining until his home and barn were destroyed by a fire in 1873.

As the community grew, tragedy visited repeatedly. Storms would blanket the region causing Preston Brook to surge, sweeping away bridges, sawmills and dwellings—and drowning multiple residents. And while the late 19th Century saw measles, fires and explosions claim the lives of multiple residents, the community continued to grow, and by 1905 the Burlington Free Press described Honey Hollow as "a thriving hamlet".

Another hardy logger making a livelihood in Honey Hollow was Fred Lafreniere, whose family moved from Altona, New York after immigrating from Canada. Working the upper valley's "Michigan Lots", Fred's son Leo would descend the mountain on his gray horse, where a lively girl named Judy—a fourth-generation Preston—would watch for him from her upstairs window. They were married in 1926.

But as the 20th Century's early decades unfolded, Honey Hollow's good fortunes changed dramatically. Lumber operations slowed as much of the land's mature timber had been harvested. The clear-cut mountainside fields left behind were steep and rocky, and even after the large glacial stones were stacked into walls, growing crops in the shady valley was a struggle. When farmers turned to sheep farming, the black bears of Camel's Hump stalked their flocks.

The original Honey Hollow Schoolhouse, c. 1944.

The Fiddock School on Duxbury Road

Mrs. O.Z. Jennings: Swept away with her husband by Preston Brook flood waters in July, 1897.

In 1913, the Muzzys sold the sprawling acreage of the old Stockwell farm to Seymour Demo, a former drummer boy in the Spanish American war. He and his wife Grace would raise six children on the farm. By 1927, few families remained in Honey Hollow, and once again only one road ascended the mountain, lined by abandoned farms and mills. Three years later, at the dawn of the Great Depression, both schools had closed for lack of students.

The 1930 census lists only the Demo family living year-round in Honey Hollow, and they too departed within several years, leasing the old Stockwell farm to tenants the Derosia family. And while the district would still be used for small logging operations into the mid-1900s, its heyday had passed. Gone was the constant sawing echoing through the hills, teams of horses dragging logs, and smoke billowing from mills and homestead chimneys. With the exception of a few seasonal hunting cabins, the cleared lands around Preston Brook were rapidly reclaimed by Green Mountain forest, hiding the abandoned settlement of Honey Hollow.

When Judy Lafreniere's father William Preston died in 1936, she and Leo returned from West Bolton to take over the farm. Leo continued the dairy operations, but never lost his true passion for logging the hills, building a sawmill just behind the homestead and selling timber to processing mills into his 70s. Judy and Leo spent the remainder of their lives in the Preston homestead that still stands today at the base of Honey Hollow Road. They were famous for their kindness and generosity, and for keeping a watchful eye on the quiet valley behind them that was once bustling with activity.

As a kid bouncing around in that old pickup truck, I didn't realize just how deep my family roots were in the region. Today, as I explore the stone cellar ruins of the old barns and farmhouses, I know the forgotten history, and more fully appreciate my ancestors and the other brave settlers who lived hard, honorable lives in Honey Hollow.

Bryan Farnsworth
Bolton History Group
February, 2021

Bolton lumbermen c. 1920s: Young Leo Lafreniere seated at left. Fred Lafreniere, with cane, seated at right.

The Preston-Lafreniere Homestead, c. 1940.

Leo & Judy (Preston) Lafreniere, c. 1920s.

Burlington Clipper.

Only $2.00 a Year.

VOL. VIII.   BURLINGTON, VT., THURSDAY, SEPTEMBER 22. 1881.   NO. 28.

Democrat Sentinel.

ESTABLISHED 1801.

VOL. LXXVIII.   BURLINGTON, VT., SATURDAY, JULY 13, 1878.   NUMBER 28.

The Waterbury Record.

VOL. XIX. NO. 33   WATERBURY, VERMONT, WEDNESDAY, NOVEMBER 19, 1913.   PRICE THREE CENTS

BURLINGTON DAILY NEWS

VOLUME 40, NUMBER 35.   BURLINGTON, VERMONT, TUESDAY, FEBRUARY 10, 1914.   10 PAGES, PRICE 2 CENTS.

Green Mountain Freeman.

VOL. XXXIX.   MONTPELIER, VT., WEDNESDAY, DECEMBER 20, 1882.   NO. 51.

Burlington Daily Free Press.

BURLINGTON, VT., FRIDAY, JULY 16, 1897.

BOLTON.—N. Streeter, lost a sheep recently, supposed to have been killed by dogs....Fred. Smith has bought a wood-lot in Honey-hollow for $9,000... Potatoes are worth 50@65 per bushel, delivered at the cars.... Sneak thieves are vigorously at work in the western part of the town. They are making raids on poultry roosts in general.

Democrat & Sentinel: Oct. 19, 1878

BOLTON.

Mrs. Sylvester Stockwell has returned home from Burlington, where she has been spending a few days with her sister, Mrs. Chambers.—Mr. and Mrs. Henry Bolles of Plainfield, visited friends in town recently.—Miss Elna Gillett is recovering from the measles. —Mr. Norman Stockwell has had the misfortune to lose a good horse recently. —Honey Hollow is struck with the measles.

Burlington Clipper - Mar. 5, 1891

The ladies Lend-a-Hand society met this week Thursday with Mrs. Musy in Honey Hollow.

Burlington Clipper - Aug. 12, 1897

A lynx was captured in a trap in that section of the town of Bolton known as Honey Hollow. It was found last Friday and had evidently been caught for several days. It measured over three feet in length and was caught by Albert Streeter of Bolton. The animal was sent to a taxidermist to be mounted. One has been seen several times this summer in the vicinity of D. L. Ring's in this town and possibly this may be the same one. However, those having seen this last mentioned one think it was a much larger animal than the one killed at Bolton.

Burlington Clipper - Nov. 3, 1900

George W. Kidder and wife, of Waterbury, went up to Bolton, walked to "Honey Hollow" and back to the depot, four miles, and picked 50 quarts of blackberries, in about six hours.

Burlington Clipper - Sep. 22, 1881

Austin Howard of Hartford, Vermont, has contracted to put 4000 cords of wood on the railroad line in Bolton from the Honey Hollow region, northwest side of Camel's Hump. He has also engaged to deliver 2,000,000 feet of spruce logs at the steam mill in Bolton, and the town is lively with lumbermen.

Green Mountain Freeman: Dec. 20, 1882

JONESVILLE.

The bears have made such havoc with Steven Hildreth's flock of sheep in Honey Hollow that he has been obliged to take them home to Jonesville. Several have been killed and the flock badly scattered. Mr Hildreth had a noble flock of sheep but the pasture is too near Camel's Hump where bears abide.

Burlington Clipper - Oct. 9, 1897

Samuel Andrews has moved one gang of his lumbermen from Joiner brook across the river to Honey Hollow brook.

Burlington Clipper - Feb. 11, 1897

BOLTON.

The remains of Mr. "Bro" Landers, who was drowned in the Preston brook in Honey Hollow on March 2, were buried in the town cemetery, March 21. The funeral services were conducted by the Rev. Mr. Holmes of Richmond, at the home of John Muzzy. The body of the drowned man was found by Carl Muzzy on March 19. His father, Lewis Landers of Essex, two brothers, Franklin of Duxbury, Hiram of Ferrisburgh, and sister, Mrs. Devoid of Starksboro, attended the services and burial, who with his mother are left to mourn his loss and untimely death. Mrs. Fleury is at work for A. W. Bohannon.

Burlington Clipper - Nov. 3, 1900

FIRST LISTER OF BOLTON DROWNED

He and His Wife Swept Down Stream – She Had Her Leg Broken.

The heavy rain of Tuesday night caused much serious damage in the town of Bolton. The roads are badly washed out, mill privileges seriously damaged. The saw mill of S. A. Andrews and other buildings, located in what is known as Honey Hollow was entirely swept away. Loss not estimated.

Mr. O. Z. Jennings, a much respected citizen, and first lister of the town was drowned in the high water in Honey Hollow. Mr. and Mrs. Jennings, both old people went down to a brook near their house to move back a large kettle. Both had hold of the utensil, when the heard a noise from above. Looking up, they saw a large tree coming down the brook, and before they could move, it had swept them in and was hurrying them down.

Both held to the tree for a time. Finally Mr. Jennings said: "I have got to go, look out for yourself." With those words he let go and the waves closed over his head.

A neighbor, Henry Muzzy, noticed that the Jennings were not about their place, and he went over. Finding nobody at the house, he went down to the brook and found Mrs. Jennings on a rock, where she had crawled, with one leg broken and otherwise terribly injured. She was cared for and search was instituted for Mr. Jennings. The body was found in some floodwood with several bruises on it. This same stream damaged Noah Preston's farm to the extent of $1000.

The funeral of Mr. Jennings will take place at 2 p. m. Friday at his late residence.

Jonesville reports that that town has not seen such a flood for 40 years. Roads are completely washed out. The farm of Dan Palmer, Will O'Neil and F. E. Briggs are ruined. The flood has also injured the pipe that brings Jonesville its supply of water.

Burlington Free Press - Jul. 16, 1897

Waterbury was enveloped in a cloud of smoke yesterday as a result of a forest fire in Honey Hollow. The terrific wind makes fighting impossible. J. L. Perkins, who owns valuable lumber tracts in Bolton, went there yesterday. The smoke from Camel's Hump is plainly seen here.

Burlington Free Press - May 17, 1903

RICHMOND

Liveryman White let a team Saturday night and loaned a fur coat to the young man having it. The man drove to Jonesville and left the coat in the sleigh. During his absence the coat was stolen. On his return he reported the facts to Mr White and the next morning they started to look the matter up. Tracks were found indicating the thief had gone into what is known as the Honey hollow section of the town of Bolton. Following the trail Mr White found his coat hidden in the attic of an unused house and later found the thief, who finally confessed to the crime and paid Mr White for his trouble.

Burlington Clipper - Jan. 9, 1904

Shocking Accident in Bolton.

A shocking accident which resulted fatally occurred Wednesday in that part of Bolton known as Honey hollow. Nellie (Raymond) Bartro was near a brush heap which her little boy had fired when her clothing took fire, and before help could arrive she was burned to death. The accident happened between 10 and 11 o'clock Wednesday forenoon. The health officer, George Pease, who is also selectman, and selectmen A. G. Stevens and N. Stockwell were notified and their verdict, rendered late in the afternoon, was accidental death. The body, wrapped in a blanket, was carried to the house about 4:30 o'clock in the afternoon.

A son, Bert Norton, who was at work in Jonesville, was notified of the accident, but did not get home until after his mother died. Two smaller boys and a little girl, by her last husband, Wesly Barto, (with whom she had not been living for two or three years) survive her. Mrs. Bartro was 48 years and seven months old. Burial was in East Bolton.

The Waterbury Record - Apr. 24, 1906

Fred Jewett has bought Mr. Coombs' farm in Honey Hollow. Mrs. Mollie Gillett and family expect to move into the hollow in the near future.—H. Muzzy was injured recently when he stepped upon the wheel of a heavy wagon and as he gave a leap the team started quickly. It was stopped before any serious damage was done.

Burlington Weekly Free Press - Sep. 23, 1915

The unoccupied buildings in Honey Hollow, known as the Foley place, also the Andrews place, situated only one-half mile apart were destroyed by fire one night last week.

F. A. Jewett of Waterbury is demolishing the house he owns in Honey Hollow and removing the lumber of the same.

Burlington Clipper - Apr. 21, 1927

Campbell & Wasson have things booming at their mill in Honey Hollow, Bolton, and have already sawed 75,000 feet of lumber. This is to be delivered at Jonesville, the rough stock coming from the lot owned by Samuel Andrews. The heavy boiler drawn from here in February is the one used at this mill for furnishing the steam power for doing the sawing. Both Mr Campbell and Mr Wasson reside in this village on Baker avenue and are evidently pushers in business matters. They will continue the lumbering business throughout the summer months.

Burlington Clipper - Apr. 30, 1904

Mrs. Thomas Trainer died at her home in "Honey Hollow" near here Wednesday, Feb. 3, after an illness of only a few hours of puerperal convulsions, aged 16 years. She left a husband and an infant son. Her remains were taken to her former home in Moretown for burial.

Waterbury Record - Feb. 16, 1909

BOLTON.

Fred Jewett and family have moved to a camp in Honey Hollow so as to be near his timber lot, where he is engaged in lumbering.—Norman Stockwell, a former resident, was in town Saturday.—The "Raymond" place in Honey Hollow which was sold at auction recently, was bid off by Dorman Stockwell of Jonesville for $100.—Mrs. Fannie Muzzy, who has been visiting relatives in Waterbury and Moretown for several weeks, has returned to the home of her son, H. Muzzy, for the winter.—Mr. and Mrs. A. C. Huntley visited at the home of her parents, Mr. and Mrs. Hayden, in Duxbury Saturday.—Mrs. Mary York and Mrs. Hannah Hardy of West Bolton visited at C. F. Sabins's Monday.—Road Commissioner Lancor is working the road on the south side of the river.

Burlington Free Press - Nov. 18, 1909

BURLINGTON, Sept. 16.—While his 21-year-old son and the entire road crew looked on, Leo Allen, 51, of St. Albans was instantly killed by a delayed dynamite explosion at Honey Hollow on the south side of the Winooski river in Bolton today.

Allen was approaching the charge for the third time to see why it didn't go off when it exploded.

The men were clearing a way to a tract of land owned by the victim's cousin, Clyde Allen.

Rutland Daily Herald - Sep. 17, 1931

The Fiddock school closed June 3 with a picnic in Honey Hollow. Mrs. Premo, who has taught there the past two years, will not return in September. Miss Iris Higley of Huntington has been engaged to take her place.

Burlington Free Press - Jun. 10, 1939

H. F. Smith of Waterbury was in Honey Hollow last week surveying lumber lands for S. A. Andrews of Richmond, who has 1,000 acres in the south part of Bolton and in Huntington. The new steam mill built and run by Wason & Campbell is located near this land, and now employs 20 men and six teams. It has built a mile of new road into the mountain and is doing a prosperous business. They will cut about one million feet per annum. Fred Jewett, who is operating the newly built mill at Bolton station, owns a large tract of lumber land adjoining Mr. Andrews lot, from which he obtains a part of his supply of logs. Altogether this is now a thriving hamlet. It will be remembered that Mr. Andrews recently sold a large tract of lumber land in the north part of Bolton which is now owned by the Torrington Brass company. He is a veteran in the business, and though now 83 years old, is as active as the average young men in the business.

Burlington Free Press - Jun. 26, 1905

KILLED DEER AFTER 5 P. M.

Charge on Which Mrs. Jewett and Her Sons are Arraigned

Burlington, Nov. 27.—Mrs. Fred A. Jewett, E. A. Jewett and F. L. Jewett her two sons and I. E. Isham, all of Richmond, were arraigned in County court today before Assistant Judge Merrihew on a charge of illegal deer killing, and admitted to bail in $100 each, surety being furnished by F. A. Jewett, husband of Mrs. Jewett.

It is charged the party killed a deer in Honey Hollow, Bolton, one day last week after 5 o'clock in the afternoon, which is contrary to law.

Bennington Evening Banner - Dec. 1, 1911

The Muzzy farm in Honey Hollow has been sold to Mr. Demo of Middlebury who takes possession March 1.

Burlington Daily News - Feb. 10, 1914

JONESVILLE

Separator Explodes in Demo Home—Two Girls Badly Cut

A separator in the home of Mr. and Mrs. S. J. Demo exploded recently, breaking dishes, sending the milk to the ceiling and throwing the dishes into the adjoining room. The separator was being operated by Alice and Rose Demo, daughters of Mr. and Mrs. Demo. The two girls were badly cut on the face and Miss Alice received a gash on her right arm.

Mrs. Ray Cagne and son, Roderick, were guests of Mr. and Mrs. Dan Larned Wednesday.

Guests at S. J. Demo's in Honey Hollow Sunday were Albert Farmer, Roosevelt Demo of West Bolton and John Demo of Waterbury.

Burlington Free Press - Apr. 6, 1934

13

Stone foundation of the Jewell sawmill on Preston Brook, 2020.

The Burlington Free Press.

VOL. 107. NO. 69.   BURLINGTON, VERMONT, SATURDAY, MARCH 21, 1942.   PRICE FOUR CENTS

U. S. Bombers Make Direct Hit On Jap Cruiser

In New Britain Harbor —Smoke Is Sent Belching From Vessel

WASHINGTON, March 20 (P)— The addition of a Japanese cruiser to the mounting total of enemy ships sunk or damaged by American army bombers in the aerial Nippon battle to forestall an invasion of Australia was reported today by the war department.

800 Miles From Their Bases

Striking at a distance of possibly 800 miles from their bases, two bombers made a direct hit on a large cruiser in the harbor of Rabaul, on the island of New Britain. Belatedly reported from General Douglas MacArthur's Australian headquarters, the attack took place Wednesday, a communique said. It followed a foray made the day before by a single long range bomber.

Burlington Man

U. S. and Chinese Troops in Tokyo, Stilwell's Goal

CHUNGKING, China, March 20. (P)—Lieut. Gen. Joseph W. Stilwell of the United States declared today that he commands all American forces in India, Burma and China in addition to the two Chinese armies in Burma, and said:

"The United States means business, and we won't be satisfied until we see American and Chinese Troops in Tokyo together."

The officer who recently became chief of staff to Chiang Kai-Shek told a press conference he was unable to go into details, "but you may assume from the fact that I have been assigned to command any United States forces in China, Burma and India that the effort contemplated is large.

"President Roosevelt has expressed his determination to use all means necessary to clear China of the Japanese."

Hitler Harassed By the Reports Of New Discord

His Own Satellites Restless—Subject Peoples in Revolt

By The Associated Press

Already throttled in the east and haunted by the specter of an allied invasion in the west, Adolf Hitler was harassed today (Saturday) by reports of mounting discord among his own "new order" satellites and by fresh revolt among Europe's subject peoples.

Potential "Third Front"

A potential "third front" was threatened in the southeast with a revival of the long-standing territorial quarrel between Hungary and Rumania, both junior partners in the Axis set-up.

Advices reaching London said the Hungarians were strengthening

MacARTHUR DECLARES PHILIPPINES WILL BE RETAKEN IN ALLIED DRIVE; CHURCHILL, CURTIN DISPUTE FLARES

Richard Casey Storm Center Of Controversy

Australia Wants Him To Remain As Minister to U. S. Britain Names Him To Empire Post

Bataan Hero's Statement Comes on a Day of Heavy Air Combat Near Australia

Centered Around Port Moresby, New Guinea—Jap Field Columns Led by Nazi Missionaries Find Going Hard

By C. YATES McDANIEL

Vermont Offers 'Sanctuary in Hills' Away from Air Raids

HERE'S SECURITY IN MOUNTAINS

The building pictured above is the new camp of Dr. and Mrs. Carl Wurm, Jr., of New York. It is constructed on a knoll in Honey Hollow, Bolton, a short distance above the camp of Mayor and Mrs. John J. Burns of Burlington. Two miles up the mountain from the Winooski River valley, the camp, located in a clearing on the old Muzzey farm, commands a sweeping view of both valleys and mountain ranges. It has been named "Open Valley Lodge."

The Honey Hollow camp site is on a 650-acre tract recently purchased by Dr. Wurm. A part of it has already been set out to 11,000 fir trees as a reforestation project. Besides the Muzzey farm, the tract also includes the old Edgar Jewett farm.

More elaborately constructed than the ordinary mountain camp, it has preserved that look of belonging to the countryside by the use of overlapping weathered-boarding for its exterior siding. The boards, along with hand-hewn timbers of decades ago and pole rafters, were utilized from the razing of an old barn on the property. It has Dutch doors. The only paint on the outside is on the window trim.

Atop the asbestos shingled roof is a small belfry housing a century-old bell picked up in Stowe. It's used to announce mealtimes. Also sticking up out of the roof is the stone chimney carrying flues from the big stone fireplace in the living room, kitchen and a furnace which has not yet been installed.

Approximately 42 by 30 feet in overall dimensions, the camp includes, besides a large living room and kitchen, two bedrooms downstairs and a loft or dormitory upstairs. The modernly equipped interior is finished in knotty pine.

In the basement is space for two cars as well as a ventilated 10-foot square concrete vault with steel door for storing valuables in the winter months or quantities of vegetables in summer.

The camp has its own running water supply and power producing plant. It was designed by Louis S. Newton, local architect, and built by Thomas Breen of Underhill.

'Safe Spots' in State Expected To Be More and More in Demand By Those in Metropolitan Areas

Refuge Possibilities Well Recognized, Good Example Being the Honey Hollow Development of Dr. Carl Wurm, Jr.

Unspoiled Vermont may become more than a favored recreation ground for residents of metropolitan areas and offer inviting refuge possibilities in the event of bombing industrial centers. Its hills and sparsely settled regions of the large cities in the northeastern section of the country.

Harold Chadwick, director of the Vermont state publicity service, yesterday disclosed that his department has received "a sprinkling" of inquiries since the United States entry into the war as to "safe spots" in Vermont.

Fear of bombings has prompted no actual new construction for refuge purposes in Vermont, as far as his department knows, Chadwick pointed out. But Dr. George D. Samson of Burlington said yesterday that a camp recently constructed by his son-in-law and daughter, Dr. and Mrs. Carl Wurm, Jr., of New York, at Honey Hollow in Bolton would serve as an ideal refuge for the family in the event New York should be subjected to air attacks.

Arthur W. Hoag, local surveyor and architect, suggested yesterday there are plans available from any number of sources for the construction of an inexpensive camp or cottage. "Plenty of land is available in Vermont, too, at a very small cost, on which to build such refuge shelters," he added. "I am surprised

the publicity service of the state has not made more of these possibilities.

"We have purposely kept away from scare advertising," explained Chadwick, "but the slogan in the spring advertising of Vermont's attractions for the summer visitor bears upon this, however — 'sanctuary in the hills.' Pointing out that there has already been a good return on this advertising campaign in the way of inquiries, he said: "There is a good demand for Vermont real estate, but whether it's normal or scarce we don't have any way of knowing."

Hoag visioned plenty of new construction from the refuge camps idea. "You wouldn't have to worry about priorities. The biggest, and almost only, item would be lumber which can be produced in our own mills from our own forests. Fireplaces could be constructed of stone. Camp stoves ought to be available. Wood could be used for fuel. I suppose the camps could even be made cozy during the cold weather months, if need be."

INTRODUCTION

Honey Hollow Camp is a remote forest property located 1800 feet up the northwestern slope of Camel's Hump in Bolton, Vermont. Nestled in the verdant glacial valley of Honey Hollow, it is known for its iconic red-roofed cabin and breathtaking views of the surrounding 21,000 unspoiled acres of Camel's Hump State Park. Established in 1941 by Carl Wurm Jr. to be a wartime sanctuary in the event his family needed to flee New York City due to a Nazi attack or invasion, it was listed on the National Register of Historic Places in 1994 to acknowledge its overall architectural merit and historic cultural significance in the context of World War II.

The Honey Hollow region was once a vibrant settlement of working farms and sawmills, and is said to have gained its moniker due to a 19th century legal dispute between residents over beehive ownership. After its year-round population plummeted in the early 1900s, left behind were just a small handful of "camps"—Vermont vernacular for private rural retreat properties. Honey Hollow Camp is the last surviving example of the valley's original recreational escapes.

Built on the site of a century-old farm homestead, the cabin was originally called "Open Valley Lodge". It was designed by architect Lewis Sheldon Newton, and is also noteworthy as an early example of salvaging and recycling materials from primitive New England barns for both their structural and aesthetic merits. The cabin's exposed axe-hewn timbers, replete with post and beam slots, give its rustic interior an 18th century charm belying its 20th century construction.

Miles away from power and telephone lines, atop a road annually rendered impassable for months by winter snow and ice, it remains an off-grid seasonal retreat isolated from the hustle and bustle of contemporary life. The cabin is situated in a ten-acre clearing surrounded by pristine Vermont hardwood forest, brimming with wild berries and abundant wildlife including deer, moose, black bear, raccoons, porcupines, bobcats and beavers. Insulated from the din of modernity, the sounds of Honey Hollow are among nature's gentlest: chirping songbirds, bumblebees, rustling leaves, and the roar of Preston Brook—teeming with trout—softly echoing through the valley.

Honey Hollow Camp has been owned by the Wooden family since 1974. This volume is a brief visual history of its founding, construction and early days, as pieced together from public records, interviews, and the Wurm family's private photographs, films and papers.

  - John A. Wooden, Summer 2021

The Old Farm viewed towards Camel's Hump. Left to right: north barn, south barn and old farmhouse, 1940.

View towards northeastern with old north barn and farmhouse at right, 1940.

THE OLD FARM

The isolated forest clearing where Honey Hollow Camp stands today was once but one field of a large farm where multiple industrious families worked the beautiful, but unforgiving landscape for over 100 years. Bolton town records suggest the Old Farm was first settled by the J. Stockwell family in the early-to-mid 1800s. Established on a sweeping 250-acre tract of land 1.8 miles up Honey Hollow Road, the farm commanded stunning views of Camel's Hump to the south and Bolton Valley to the north from its high, flat perch between Robin's Mountain & Bald Mountain.

The homestead was a classic New England "connected farm": a two-story "big house" with living quarters attached to the one-story "little house" kitchen area with a front porch. Behind both was the "back house", consisting of multiple smaller structures for keeping wagons, small livestock, and an outhouse. Directly across the road, two large post-and-beam barns and a granary were the center of farming operations, encircled by at least 30 acres of sloping fields and pasture.

The property was active for over a century with dairy, maple syrup and apple production, as well as logging for cord wood and lumber. At least two generations of Stockwells worked the land before it was sold to the J.W. and Frannie Muzzy family in 1899. Their son Carl would later sell it to the S. J. Demo family in 1913. The Derosias were the last family to occupy the farm year-round, as tenants, into the 1940s. Potato crops planted in 1942-1944 marked the final years of Honey Hollow agriculture.

The two largest barns and "back house" buildings were dismantled in 1941 to build Honey Hollow Camp, and the remaining structures including the farmhouse were razed in 1950. After farming ceased, forest quickly reclaimed most of the fields. Today, only around ten acres remain clear, and the big house's front steps, a mile of stone walls, and a small patch of perennial day lilies are the last visual remnants of the Old Farm.

Westward view of the old farmhouse & granary, 1945.

The old farmhouse, c. 1930s. (Identity of child unknown.)

Muzzy Carl & John
To Demo S. J.

Know all men by these presents that we, Carl E. Muzzy and Ella B. Muzzy - husband and wife - and J. W. Muzzy - father of said Carl E. Muzzy (J. W. Muzzy of Bolton) of Waterbury in the County of Washington and State of Vermont, in the consideration of Fourteen hundred dollars paid to our full satisfaction by S. J. Demo & D. J. Demo husband & wife, of Middlebury, in the County of Addison and State of Vermont by these presents do freely give, grant, sell, convey and confirm unto the said S. J. & D. J. Demo and their heirs and assigns forever, a certain piece of land in Bolton, in the County of Chittenden and State of Vermont, described as follows, viz:

Being all and the same land and premises conveyed to the said Carl E. Muzzy by J. W. & Fannie S. Muzzy by Warranty deed dated October 8-1906, recorded in Book 16 pages 345 & 346 of Bolton Land Records - being what was formerly known as the Stockwell farm and supposed to contain about 150 acres more or less. And we also for the same consideration include in this conveyance all the hay in the south lay in the large barn on the premises. We also hereby convey for the same consideration all of lots #138 & 139 in said Bolton, situate on the south side of the Winooski river and adjoining the farm above described which was conveyed to said Carl E. Muzzy by Lorman Stockwell by deed dated April 3rd 1899 recorded in Vol. 15 page 145 of Bolton Land Records. Said lots containing 100 acres, more or less.

In Witness whereof we hereunto set our hands and seals this 20th day of Sept. A. D. 1913

In presence of   Carl E. Muzzy

L. A. Babcock   Ella B. Muzzy

James R. Fullerton   John W. Muzzy

1913 deed transfer from Carl E. Muzzy to S. J. Demo (Detail).

View southeast towards Camel's Hump with north barn, south barn and granary, 1940.

Connected farm outbuildings behind farmhouse with southeast view of Camel's Hump, 1940.

View eastward towards Bald Mountain from behind the "connected farm" homestead, 1940.

View southeast towards Camel's Hump with south barn and granary (corn barn) at left, 1940.

Front Steps to the Old Farmhouse, Summer 2021

Photo: John A. Wooden

Old Farm Stone Walls, Spring 2021

Photo: Jennifer Wooden Mitchell

Old Farm Stone Walls, Fall 2018

Photo: Ken Wooden

From left, Dr. Carl Wurm Jr., Edith Samson Wurm, Edie Wurm, Mabel Samson & Dr. George Samson, 1941

THE WURM ESTATE

By 1940, Honey Hollow lay peaceful and largely deserted. Across the Atlantic, World War II was engulfing Europe, and just 300 miles south, New York City residents grew increasingly fearful over news reports of Nazi U-Boats prowling just off the east coast.

Dr. Carl Wurm, Jr., an affluent general practitioner physician living in the Bronx, was among many anxious city-dwellers who began making contingency plans for their families to flee the Big Apple in the event the war came to America. Carl's wife Edith Samson Wurm was born and raised in Burlington, Vermont—where the Wurms traveled regularly with their young daughter Edie to visit her grandparents, Dr. George and Mabel Samson.

Deciding the Green Mountain State was the natural destination should they need to evacuate New York, the Wurms asked Dr. Samson, a native Vermonter, to keep an eye peeled for suitable properties. Affable and social, George Samson practiced dentistry for many years from his Main Street office in Burlington. He owned one of the first automobiles in Vermont, enabling him to visit people far and wide, and become highly familiar with Chittenden County's many tucked-away locales.

Eager to help ensure the safety of his only daughter's family, Dr. Samson dove into a months-long search for available local real estate. In the fall of 1940, he spotted an advertisement for a large tract of land for sale in Honey Hollow. Following an inquiry, he made a preliminary visit to the Old Farm. It was remote, scenic, and inexpensive—perfect for his son-in-law's planned wartime escape.

Samson alerted Wurm, who booked a seat on the ski train to Vermont to survey the spot...

Farms
Lake and Mountain
Properties
Town and Country
Homes

Vermont Realty Service

John J. Gagnon, Mgr.

Room 4 - 203 Main Street

BURLINGTON, -:- VERMONT

Industrial Plants
Hotels
Country Stores
Gas Stations
Tourists Cabins

October 9, 1940

George D. Samson
600 East 164th St.
New York City

Dear Sir:

    In reply to your letter of October 8, the 400 acres advertised in the New York paper is located in the town of Bolton, two miles from Jonesville and a railroad station. It is only half a mile over a good dirt road to the main highway. The elevation is about 1800 feet with beautiful mountain views.

    There are 40 acres of good rich tillable land, and it is watered by good brooks and springs. The price is cash as this is a very unusual bargain. It is estimated to cut about ten thousand cords of wood with a good ready market at the road side. The property is not mortgaged and the title is clear.

    Enclosed you will find a booklet of other Vermont properties which I think will interest you. May we hear from you soon?

        Yours very respectfully,

        VERMONT REALTY SERVICE, INC.

        John J. Gagnon

        John J. Gagnon, Mgr.

SEARCH FOR U-BOATS OFF NEW ENGLAND

Naval and Coast Guard Ships, Aided by Planes, Join Patrol

Special to THE NEW YORK TIMES.

BOSTON, Sept. 23—Coast guard and naval vessels, with orders to intercept any craft from American ports carrying oil to U-boats, patrolled the North Atlantic today in seach of a possible contact point between short craft and submersibles.

Armed planes aided in the coverage of several hundred miles of New England coastal waters in which President Roosevelt has announced that alien submarines had been sighted. There have also been reports that U-boats have attempted to attack fishing craft for food.

Dr. George Samson drives, c. "Early 1900s"

Dr. Carl Wurm Jr. standing on the future site of the Honey Hollow Camp cabin, November 1940.

On November 29, 1940, the day after Thanksgiving, Carl Wurm, George Samson and his good friend Ralph Holmes hitched a ride up the valley on the horse-drawn sleigh of Leo Lafreniere, who lived at the base of Honey Hollow Road. Bundled in wool coats and heavy boots, the group explored and photographed the snow-draped Old Farm, evaluated sightlines of the glorious mountain views, and enjoyed coffee and a chilly lunch on the vacant farmhouse's front porch. Smitten by Honey Hollow's beauty, Wurm deputized his father-in-law to buy the Old Farm on his behalf from S.J. Demo for $700—even before Mrs. Wurm had seen it. A few months later, he also purchased a larger adjoining parcel to the north which contained the old Jewett, Raymond and Andrews farms, creating a 650-acre estate on which to build his secluded sanctuary.

Dr. Wurm, 1940.

Professor Holmes, 1940.

Carl Wurm Jr., George Samson (pointing north) and Leo Lafreniere with Camel's Hump in background, November 1940.

Leo Lafreniere & Dr. Samson look on as Dr. Wurm points eastward with Stimson Mountain in background, November 1940.

Know all Men by these Presents:

That I S. J. Demo

of Waterbury in the County of Washington and State of Vermont in the consideration of Seven hundred ($700.00) Dollars paid to my full satisfaction by George D. Samson

of Burlington in the County of Chittenden and State of Vermont by these presents, do freely give, grant, sell, convey and confirm unto the said George D. Samson

and his heirs and assigns forever, a certain piece of land in Bolton in the County of Chittenden and State of Vermont, described as follows, viz.:

Being the same land and premises with the buildings thereon standing that were conveyed to S. J. Demo and G. J. Demo (said G. J. Demo now deceased) by Carl E. Munzer, Ella Munzer and John W. Munzer by their deed of Warranty dated the 20th day of September A. D. 1913 said deed of record in Vol 16. at page 865-866 of the land records of the Town of Bolton.

Meaning to convey by this deed all the land and premises which I the said S. J. Demo own in the Town of Bolton and being situated on the Southerly side of the Winooski River in that part of said Town commonly called "Honey Hollow" supposed to contain two hundred fifty acres. (250.) to be the same more or less.

Reference is hereby made to the above mentioned deed. to the record thereof and to all deeds and records therein referred to for a more particular description.

To Have and to Hold said granted premises, with all the privileges and appurtenances thereof, to the said George D. Samson his heirs and assigns, to their own use and behoof forever, and I the said S. J. Demo for myself and my heirs, executors and administrators, do covenant with the said George D. Samson his heirs and assigns, that until the ensealing of these pr[...] of the premises and have good right and title to convey the same in manner aforesaid; that [...] hereby engage to warrant and defend the same against all lawful claims whatever.

In Witness Whereof I hereunto set my hand and seal this [...]

In presence of

F. A. Phillips

[illegible] Demo

S. J. [...]

State of Vermont, Chittenden County, ss. } At Bolton this [...] day of [...]

S. J. Demo

personally appeared and acknowledged this instrument by him sealed and subscribed, to be his free act and deed.

Before me, F. A. Phillips Notary Public

Bolton Town Clerk's Office, Feb 3rd A. D. 1941, at 8th o'clock, minutes A. M.

Received the deed of which the foregoing is a true record.

Attest, F. A. Phillips Town Clerk.

Bolton Vt. 2-3rd 1941

Received from Geo. D. Samson

One & 25/100 Dollars

Recording Demo deed and searching records

$1.25 F. A. Phillips T. C.

McAuliffe Paper Company Inc. Stationers, Burlington, Vt.

Deed of sale from S.J. Demo to Dr. George Samson for $700.

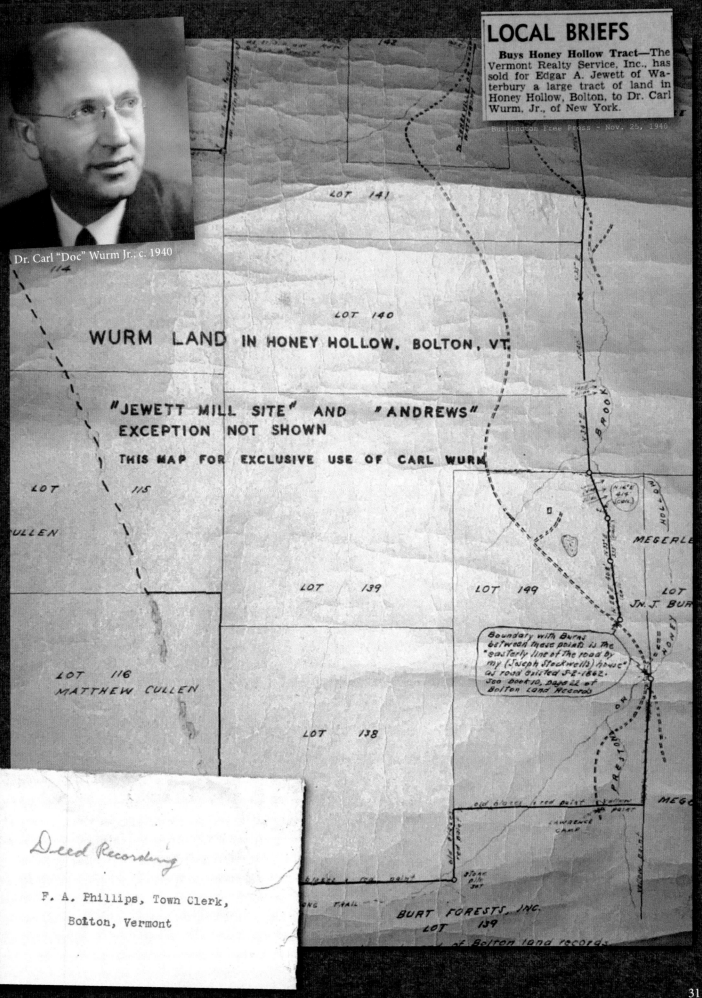

Dr. Carl "Doc" Wurm Jr., c. 1940

LOT 142

LOT 141

114

LOT 140

WURM LAND IN HONEY HOLLOW, BOLTON, VT.

"JEWETT MILL SITE" AND "ANDREWS"
EXCEPTION NOT SHOWN

THIS MAP FOR EXCLUSIVE USE OF CARL WURM

LOT 115

CULLEN

MEGERLE

LOT 139

LOT 149

JN. J. BUR

LOT
LOT 116
MATTHEW CULLEN

Boundary with Burns between these points is the "easterly line of the road by my (Joseph Stockwell's) house" as road existed 5-2-1862. See Book 10, page 22 of Bolton Land Records

LOT 138

PRESTON

HONEY

old blazes & red point

MEGO

LAWRENCE CAMP

Deed Recording

F. A. Phillips, Town Clerk,
Bolton, Vermont

STONE PILE SET

LONG TRAIL

BURT FORESTS, INC.
LOT 139

of Bolton land records

31

Spring Thaw, 2021

Photo: Jennifer Wooden Mitchell

Photo: Ken Wooden

Honey Hollow Road, Autumn 2018

LOUIS SHELDON NEWTON, ARCHITECT

"When people of prominence wanted work done, they called him."

— Martha Knapp, Hartford Historical Society

Dr. Wurm commissioned the sought-after Burlington architect Louis Sheldon Newton (1871-1953) to produce three possible designs for his mountain retreat. A Vermont native, Newton studied his trade in Boston before enjoying a fruitful, nearly 60-year career in his home state. While his specialty was alterations of existing buildings, Newton also produced original designs for residential, municipal and commercial projects—many in the Colonial Revival style. In addition to summer camps, his prodigious and eclectic output included homes, apartment buildings, banks, a hotel, a public library, faculty housing at Dartmouth College, a windmill, one of Sears & Roebuck's famous kit houses, the Tip Top bread factory in White River Junction, and even a lavish dog house commissioned by Shelburne Museum founder Electra Havemeyer Webb, of the Vanderbilt family. Newton worked until the year before he died.

Photo: UVM library

Architect Lewis Sheldon Newton

SPECIFICATIONS
FOR

*a CAMP —
DR. CARL WURM*

L. S. NEWTON
ARCHITECT
BURLINGTON, VERMONT

SPECIFICATIONS

OF THE LABOR AND MATERIAL required
in the Erection and Completion of

A CAMP FOR

DR. CARL WURM of New York City

HONEY HOLLOW, BOLTON, Vermont

Commission No. 725

- - - - - - - -

Louis Sheldon Newton
ARCHITECT

135 St. Paul Street, Burlington

DR. CARL WURM JR.
600 EAST 164TH STREET
NEW YORK

DR. CARL WURM JR.
600 EAST 164TH STREET
NEW YORK

1 Local gravel & sand must be OK by architect
before it is used

2. Forms - do we furnish new or old lumber

3. Concrete - If gravel is not OK for use,
size of broken stone must be specified

4. Instead of poured concrete foundation would not
cement block foundation be cheaper.

5. Back fill should be tamped and watered as
filling progresses.

6. Rough flooring to be laid diagonally, furnish
floor across floor Beams. This applies to
1st floor only.

7. Vapor seal Celotex - why cannot we furnish
this also. I can check the dealers price through
the A.P. Direct to

8. Why cannot we also furnish the windows
buying them from local lumber Dealer.

9. Cylinder locks too expensive

10. Asphalt shingles OK. Strip shingles
with extra heavy butts.

11. Flooring of Fir not Oak.

12. Recess the medicine cabinet between 2
studs setting out one as shown.

13 Stock screen doors & 16 wire

60.00 Shingles
90.00 Siding
roof
42
12
84
42
50
60
750

42
156
672
240
280
1152
1000
152

1000

Left: L.S. Newton architectural
specifications folder cover.
Above: Final architectural
specifications title page.
Right: Dr. Wurm's notes on materials.

DESIGN #1

Newton's first design represented a somewhat bare-bones take on a gentleman's hunting lodge. With a single floor and modestly sloping roofline, the ostensibly rustic cabin featured a modern kitchen and bath, and oversized windows for appreciating the site's spectacular wilderness views. Three outdoor porches—two covered and one exposed—could accommodate small open-air gatherings. Indoors, a "Gun Room" foyer set the theme upon entry, and a sense of fraternal camaraderie prevailed over privacy, with exposed communal flop bunks in lieu of bedrooms, and the large main room dominated by a fireplace and central wet bar for serving up après-hunt spirits.

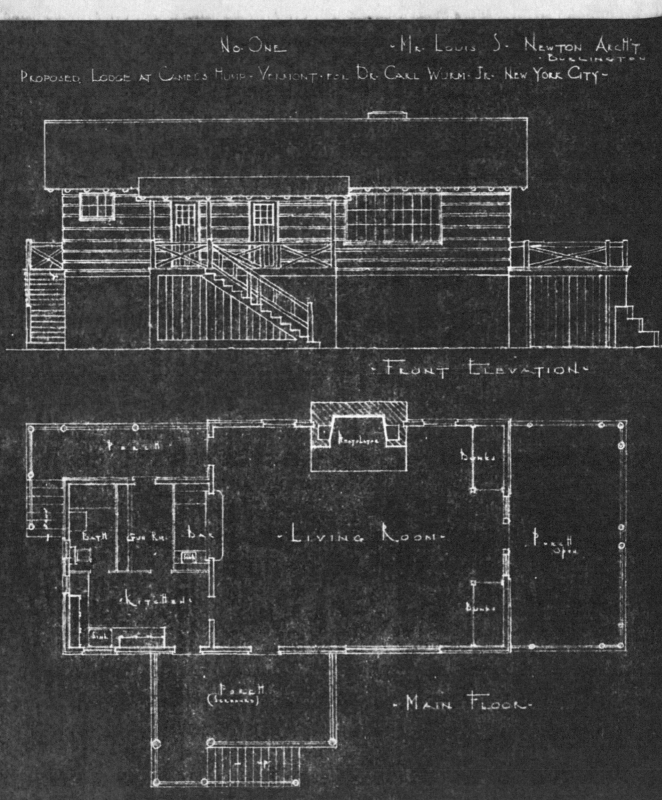

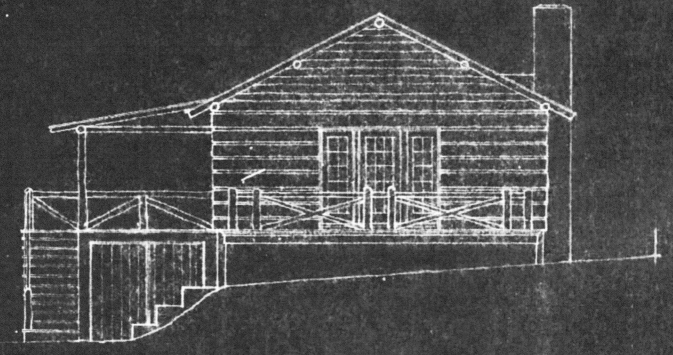

·End Elevation·

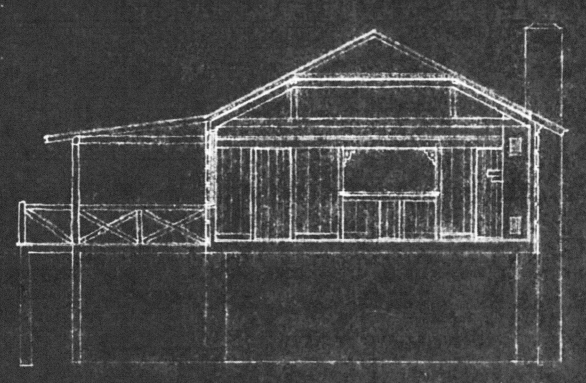

·Section·

Scale ¼" : 1'0

DESIGN #2

Design #2 was a considerably more grand affair. With a prominent belfry perched atop a large, steep roof, the cabin's footprint and overall square footage increased dramatically with the addition of both a second floor and attached two-car garage. To accommodate more guests, the main room and two outdoor porches were enlarged, with both the latter covered. And while the open, high-ceiling living room preserved the first design's sense of community, its built-in bunks were reduced to two from four, and the wet bar was downgraded to a dry bar. The addition of a proper bedroom on the first floor, along with sleeping space in a second floor loft, ensured private space.

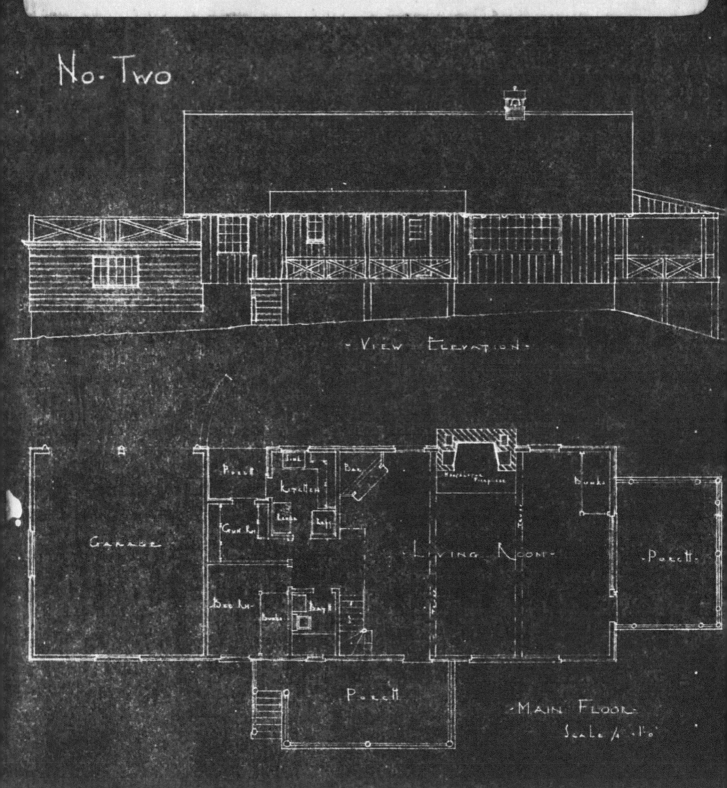

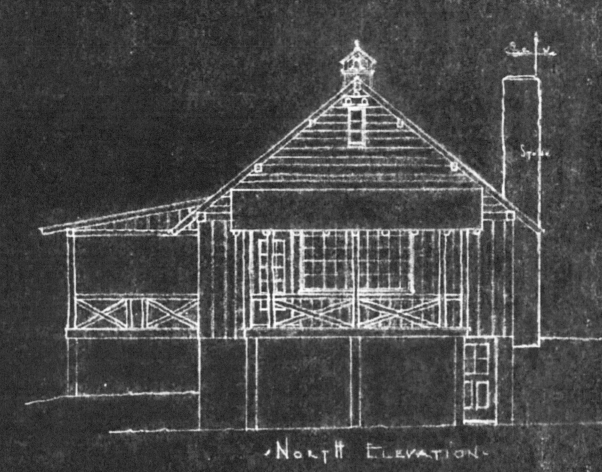

· NORTH ELEVATION ·

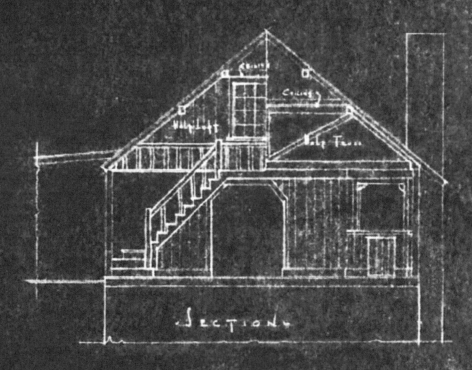

· SECTION ·

· PROPOSED · LODGE · AT · CAMEL'S HUMP · VERMONT ·
FOR
· DR · CARL · WURM · JR · · NEW YORK CITY ·
MR · LOUIS · S · NEWTON · ARCHITECT ·
· JAN 31 1914 · · BURLINGTON VERMONT ·

DESIGN #3

The preservation of a "Gun Room" and two living room bunks notwithstanding, Lewis' third design shed most hunting lodge trappings in favor of a more domestic layout better suited for year-round, co-ed entertaining. Design #2's belfry and steeper roofline now came perched atop a considerably smaller, squarish, but more efficient layout that relocated the two-car garage to the cellar. The addition of a second bedroom on the first floor reduced the great room's share of the structure's footprint, enabling the creation of a larger upstairs loft to maximize sleeping space. While not without a few compromises—in particular its lack of the other designs' grand outdoor porches—this more refined, house-like cabin was the Wurms' final choice for their wartime refuge.

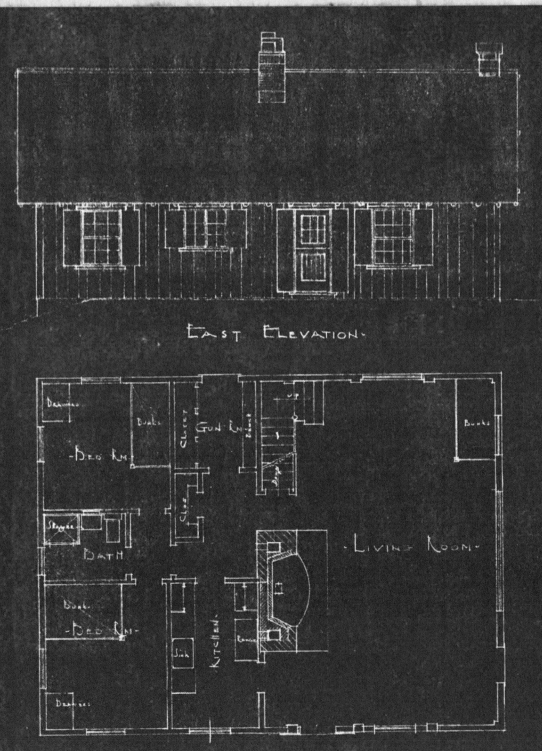

EAST ELEVATION·

·FIRST FLOOR PLAN·

CAMP AT HONEY HOLLOW
BOLTON · VERMONT· FOR
DR· CARL WURM
NEW YORK CITY·
COM·NO·725 SHEET NO·2·
SCALE ¼"=1'-0
MR· LOUIS S· NEWTON
·ARCHITECT·
·BURLINGTON·VERMONT·
G
2

· NORTH ELEVATION·

· SOUTH ELEVATION·

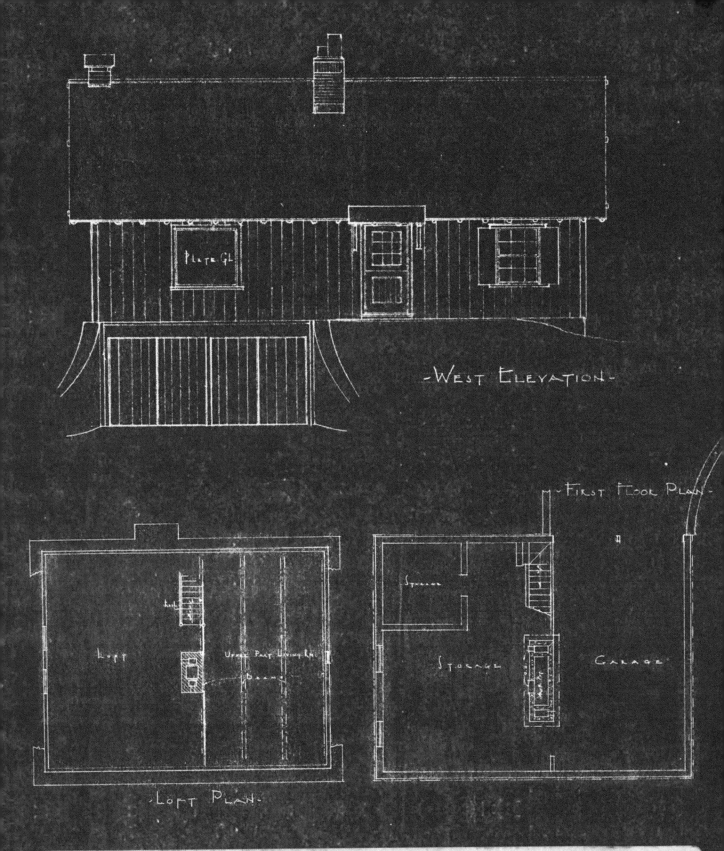

-WEST ELEVATION-

Plate Gl.

-FIRST FLOOR PLAN-

-LOFT PLAN-

Loft

Upper Part Living Rm.

Space

Storage

Garage

ALTERATIONS

Before breaking ground, the Wurms requested various modifications to Newton's final design; the gabled roofline was further steepened, the north-facing "picture window" was pushed out several feet to create a nook, and the garage entrance was moved out of sight to the cabin's east side. Banished altogether were the great room's built-in bunks. One bespoke addition was "the vault"—a cellar storage room of reinforced concrete walls and ceiling, outfitted with a heavy steel door.

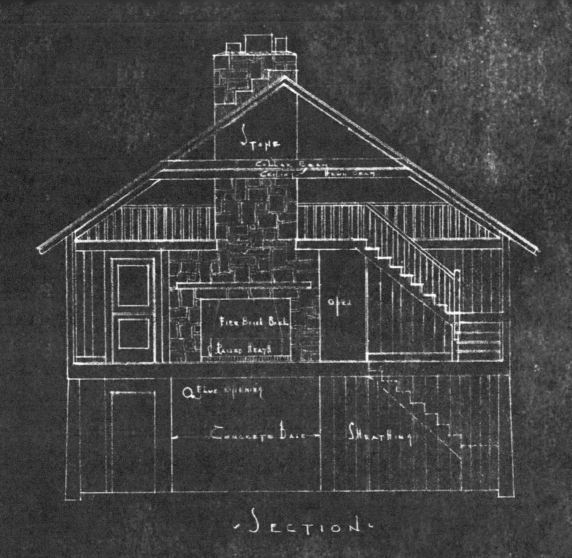

·SECTION·

·SOUTH ELEVATION·

CONSTRUCTION

Construction of Honey Hollow Camp commenced in the spring of 1941, with the Old Farm's meadows still dappled with patches of melting snow. Dr. Wurm hired his new neighbor Leo Lafreniere to complete two essential jobs: dismantling the large post-and-beam barns and outbuildings, and digging the cabin's foundation.

Leo recalled the demolition of the barns in a 1993 interview, explaining how he'd "skid the timbers down from the old barn and knock the pins out of them" before carefully stacking them for reuse in building the cabin's frame. "Didn't take me too long. I had a couple helpers", Lafreniere remembered. Of one helper named Earl Clark he recounted, "He'd go up there on the top of the building and dance on the beams—scared me to death!"

Also recycled were the old barns' exterior rough-cut pine boards, beautifully weathered by decades of exposure to the seasons, for use as the new cabin's rustic siding. Only the best boards were selected however, with many deemed too deteriorated. Leo recalled needing to make a special trip to Underhill to purchase additional old barn siding needed to finish the job.

In digging the cabin's foundation, Leo enlarged upon an extant cellar hole from a previous structure that once stood on the same spot. He used a large horse-drawn steel scoop with long wooden handles. The horse would drag the scoop in concentric circles, scraping up layers of dirt, which Leo would dump wheelbarrow-style away from the hole before returning to make additional passes. Asked what he charged Wurm, Lafreniere replied "$3 a day—man and team".

Primary construction of the camp continued through the summer as per the detailed specifications of architect L.S. Newton. The contractors were Thomas Breen of Underhill (general) and John M. Wilbur of Burlington (plumbing). Other local workers included Kenneth Preston, Mylar Laflin and his son. The cabin was completed in the autumn of 1941—just weeks prior to the Japanese attack on Pearl Harbor, which confirmed Dr. Wurm's worst fears about the war coming to America.

SCOPE OF THE WORK:

    The work is intended to cover the Mason and Carpenter work necessary to construct the building. Starting with the foundations and including the erection of a stone fireplace and chimney and other mason work; and the using of certain second-hand lumber salvaged by wrecking of the barns that were on the property, for outside wall covering and finish and exposed rafters and beams and other framing, as found to be practical; and new material as may be necessary and concealed. New windows, doors, inside sheathing and other trim will be furnished by the Contractor as necessary to complete the building as hereinafter described. The second-hand materials are piled near the site and may be seen upon inspection of the location. The Contractor should familiarize himself with the location.

L.S. Newton Architectural Specification (Detail)

Stacks of salvaged barn boards lie along Honey Hollow Road as the north barn is dismantled, Spring 1941.

Leo Lafreniere, 1941

Dr. Samson surveys demolition of old farm's back buildings.

Cabin foundation under construction beyond Dr. Wurm's 1938 Cadillac Sixty Special, May 1941.

Dr. Carl Wurm Jr., Dr. George Samson & Professor Ralph Holmes atop foundation framing, May 1941.

EXCAVATION:

Remove the loam for a distance of at least 15' outside the batten boards and place in a convenient location as directed. Excavate for basement, foundations, footings, trenches, etc., as may be necessary to carry out the plans. All footings are to be to a depth of at least 4'-6" below the finished grade line in all cases. All materials so removed are to be deposited for the rough grading as directed. If the sand and gravel is found satisfactory to use in concrete or mortar, the Contractor may so use it as far as he finds it practical.X All grading material to be smoothed and left in neat condition.

X and its quality has been passed by owner or his representative

FORMS:

Construct wood forms to hold the concrete of sizes required thoroughly bracing and tieing them to ensure no spreading and a straight and plumb wall when removed. Lumber for the forms will be supplied by the Owner and may be used in the construction. The Contractor to use care in removing them and cleaning the material.

New lumber or old siding? on hand

Foundation framing. Pictured: Dr. Samson, Prof. Holmes, Edie Wurm, Edith Wurm, Mary Holmes & Mabel Samson, May 1941.

Summer Storm Clouds, 2008

FOUNDATIONS AND FOOTINGS:

The Contractor is to construct footings and foundations, including the chimney base to the floor line, of solid concrete, of sizes, thickness and heights shown on the plans. Leave all forms on until the contrete is thoroughly set.

CONCRETE:

All concrete is to be Standard 1-2-4 Concrete Institute Specification and must be thoroughly mixed in a power mixer, and poured without break. *Size of broken stone if used should be stated – unnecessary if gravel is used*

L.S. Newton Architectural Specification (Detail)

Professor Ralph Holmes & Dr. George Samson sit atop "the vault" basement reinforced concrete storage room, May 1941.

VAULT DOOR:

The Owner will supply the iron vault door in the basement but this Contractor is to set same and pour in the concrete to make it intregal with the wall. Also provide base and ceiling vents as directed. Ceiling of the vault to be 4" concrete slab reinforced.

L.S. Newton Architectural Specification (Detail)

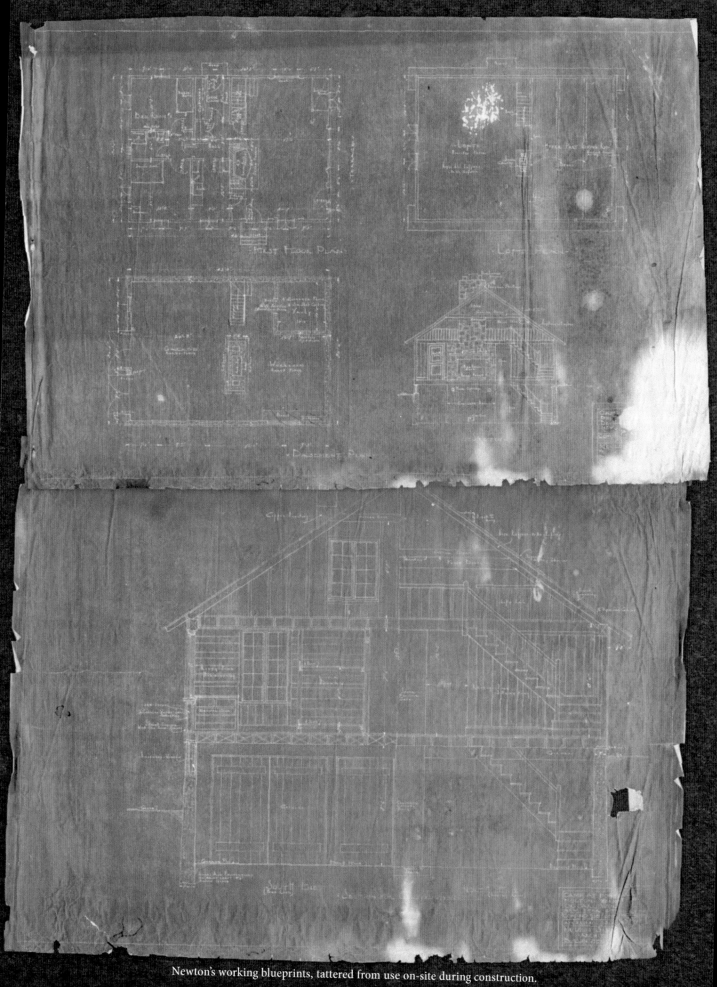

Newton's working blueprints, tattered from use on-site during construction.

Dr. Wurm poses outside the cabin frame of salvaged barn posts & beams, with fireplace stones at right, Summer 1941.

FRAMING:

The building is to be framed by using the heavy hand hewn beams now on the property for sills, plates, posts, rafters, false beams, etc., as directed. The dressed 2" joists will be used for the support of the first floor as practical and new lumber will be supplied by the Owner for the remainder. All studding both for exterior and interior walls will be new. All material is to be carefully selected, cut and handled to insure as little damage as possible and as little waste using the best portion of the beams, as directed. All to be thoroughly and securely nailed and framed in the best manner.

Floor over Garage to be framed and supported as may be governed by material furnished by Owner.

BOARDING:

All floor boards for the first floor will be new. Roof boards and loft flooring will be matched and supplied by the Owner. Sheathing on the roof is to have the best side exposed in the rooms. All to be thoroughly nailed at every bearing. *Rough floors to be laid diagonaly - finished floor across floor beams - this refers to first floor only.*

Southeast corner of cabin framing, Summer 1941.

Cabin northern facade framing, Summer 1941.

A MIGHTY HEARTH

Honey Hollow Camp's signature interior feature is its enormous stone fireplace and three-flue chimney. A twelve-foot wide exposed column of masonry towering 30+ feet high, the fireplace is positioned centrally to heat the entire cabin, with an oversized firebox designed to contain roaring infernos made of logs up to four feet long. On the north side, a small wooden frame was inlaid on which to hang a large bull moose head, one of Dr. Wurm's big game trophies.

As for the fireplace stones themselves, not just any would do. While countless suitable rocks lay strewn by glaciers for convenient collection just yards away in nearby Homestead or Preston Brooks—or atop the old walls crisscrossing his property—Dr. Wurm was more selective.

Three years earlier, when the hurricane of 1938 turned Preston Brook into a violent torrent, many stones rolled down the mountain in its powerful current. Some came to rest in the flat area south of the Winooski River, just steps from the turnoff to Honey Hollow Road. It was here that Dr. Wurm's eye was caught by the stones sparkling in a sunny stretch of brook passing through Leo Lafreniere's big meadow.

Leo Lafreniere being interviewed in 1993.

"He wanted them stones because the minerals in them—because they were shiny", Lafreniere explained in a 1993 interview. And so it was that Wurm hired Leo a third time in 1941, to haul the iridescent stones up the hill for his planned magnificent fireplace. "I had an old Chevrolet dump truck four cylinder. I was glad to do it", recalled Leo. "Money was pretty slim in those days."

Chimney construction approaches the roofline, with terra cotta flue lining protruding, Summer 1941.

FLORA OF HONEY HOLLOW

Northern facade is enclosed as the fireplace chimney approaches the roofline.

Northern facade is partially clad as enclosure of the roof begins.

The old farm's granary still stands as the camp's exterior walls take shape.

OUTSIDE WALLS:

The exterior walls to the eave line are to be sheathed by lapping the boards; and the gable ends by using the boards with clapboard effect. The old exterior boarding from the building demolished are to be used.

OUTSIDE FINISH:

All outside finish and trim to be of the old material and used as directed.

L.S. Newton Architectural Specification (Detail)

WINDOWS:

Provide Anderson or Curtis Standard Casement Windows complete with 18 mesh copper screens, in wood frames, weatherstriped and with bronze hardware and Rotary operator for all windows so indicated. All to be of stock sizes as shown. Provide standard cellar windows for all openings in the basement as indicated. Provide stationary 1-3/4" pine sash with plank frames for the plate glass and other stationary sash as shown. *Why not try some of your Canadian Lumber?*

SHINGLES:

Supply and apply heavy Asphalt shingles on the roof, allowing the sum of $7.50 per square for them, delivered on the sit

CITY MOUSE, COUNTRY MOUSE

In the summer of 1941, Dr. Wurm's daughter Edie and Leo Lafreniere's son Ronnie were both four years old. While grownups built the cabin, the outgoing little girl from the Bronx and the shy fifth-generation Preston boy became friends. Playing for long hours amongst piles of lumber and dirt, they beat the heat with ice-cold bottles of Coke, and at day's end, Edie implored, "Please stay, Ronnie".

THE BELL

Honey Hollow Camp's iconic rooftop belfry may appear merely ornamental, but it served an important functional purpose. The large brass bell, sourced by Dr. Wurm from a century-old retired steam locomotive, echoes powerfully through the valley, and was rung at mealtimes to summon those who were too far away to hear verbal calls to supper shouted from the cabin.

South facade with partial exterior cladding and belfry framing.

BELFRY:

        Construct a small belfry on the south end, make same to
fit the bell provided by the Owner. Shingle the roof
the same shingles used on the roof.

L.S. Newton Architectural Specification (Detail)

CHIMNEY:

Construct chimney, with concrete base to the first floor line and from there to above the roof, as shown, of field stone which may be gathered from about the premises, selecting same and especially those for the fireplace facing in the living room. Leave openings on all floors as shown for stoves, setting heavy galvanized iron thimbles of sizes directed. Line the chimney from just below the first floor line its entire height with terra cotta flue linings, leaving projecting at the top as indicated. Liners to be of sizes shown. Construct fireplace lining and the underfire of standard fire brick and provide the necessary cast iron throat and damper, ash dump and angle iron for support of the arch. Provide clean-out doors in the basement as shown. Clean all stone and brick and leave ready to use. All stone and brick to be laid in a strong cement mortar. The hearth is to be of flat stones gathered from the premises.

INTERIOR FINISH:

Wainscoting

All rooms on the main floor are to be finished in Knotty pine as follows: The Living room is to have a 30" dado of the old gray boards and vertical Colonial Matched Knotty Pine sheathing to the ceiling and to be finished with a chair rail and cornice. The kitchen and bath and hall are to be sheathed with vertical knotty pine. The chambers and gun room to have a knotty pine dado about 30" high with the same material applied vertically to the ceiling. Finish with chair rail and small cornice. All rooms to have base. No kitchen cupboard, closet trim, bunks, or bookcases are to be built under this contract. Window stools and trim as well as other finish necessary are to be of knotty pine. Sheath the ceiling under collar girts over the Living Room with Knotty pine as above specified.

FLOORING:

All flooring on the first floor, except the living room, is to be 2-1/2" face red oak, First Grade, carefully laid, smoothed and left ready for the painter to finish. Floor may be laid before partitions are erected, if desired, but must be thoroughly protected. The Living room floor is to be pine of wide boards, carefully nailed and plugged with false plugs as directed. This flooring will be furnished by the Owner.

Honey Hollow Camp Interior, c. 1942.

Dr. Wurm painting shutters.

The Samsons & Wurms, 1941

Professor Holmes builds a rope railing for stone rear steps.

Edith and Edie Wurm rake the lawn before planting grass.

Installing the belfry rope.

Edie Wurm at play beside unfinished power plant.

Autumn, 1941

Autumn, 1941

Homestead Brook a.k.a. Honey Hollow Stream, 2019

Photo: Grant Mitchell

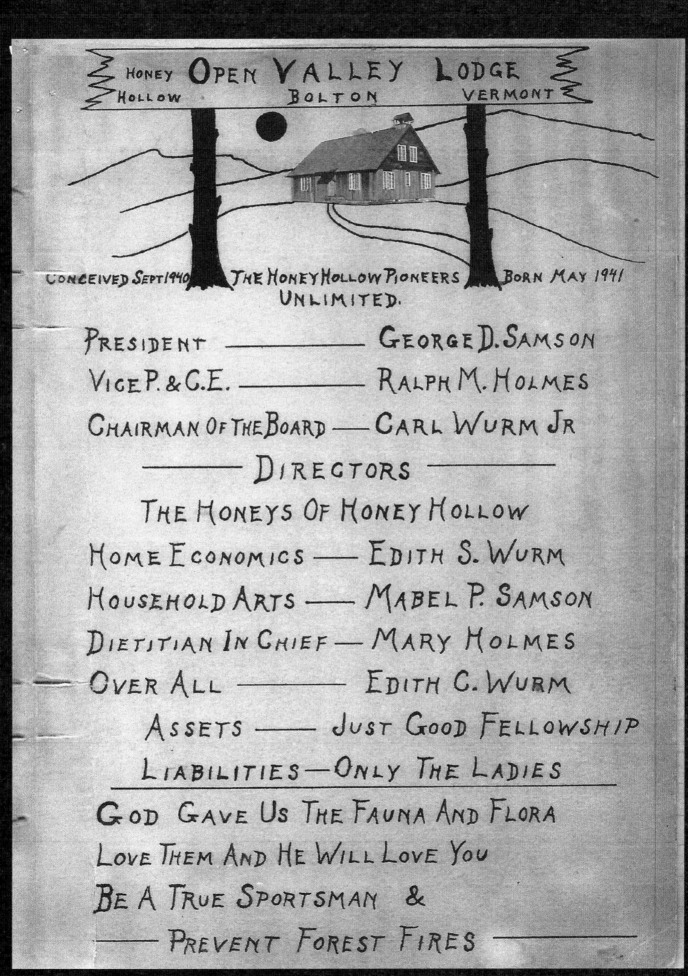

OPEN VALLEY LODGE

HONEY HOLLOW   BOLTON   VERMONT

CONCEIVED SEPT 1940   THE HONEY HOLLOW PIONEERS   BORN MAY 1941
UNLIMITED.

PRESIDENT ——————— GEORGE D. SAMSON

VICE P. & C.E. ——————— RALPH M. HOLMES

CHAIRMAN OF THE BOARD —— CARL WURM JR

———————— DIRECTORS ————————

THE HONEYS OF HONEY HOLLOW

HOME ECONOMICS —— EDITH S. WURM

HOUSEHOLD ARTS —— MABEL P. SAMSON

DIETITIAN IN CHIEF —— MARY HOLMES

OVER ALL ——————— EDITH C. WURM

ASSETS —— JUST GOOD FELLOWSHIP

LIABILITIES —— ONLY THE LADIES

GOD GAVE US THE FAUNA AND FLORA

LOVE THEM AND HE WILL LOVE YOU

BE A TRUE SPORTSMAN &

—— PREVENT FOREST FIRES ——

View of Open Valley Lodge facing southeast from "Birch Cross Cliff" high on the western ridge of Honey Hollow.

VERMONT MOUNTAIN LIVING

Once the cabin was completed, the Wurms settled into an annual schedule, spending the entire month of July in Honey Hollow—plus the holiday week between Christmas and New Years.

Summers were a refreshing departure from their New York City lives, if not exactly restful; the Wurms didn't have servants and did much of the labor to maintain the camp themselves. Their daughter Edie recalls her mother working harder in July than any other month, occupied with family, cooking, hand-washing laundry and housekeeping. When not mowing or clearing the always-encroaching brush, Dr. Wurm loved to tinker, woodwork, and drive his Jeep.

They hosted friends and family regularly; the Samsons and the Holmes were frequent guests, often dining al fresco in warm weather to enjoy the beautiful scenery. Most guests lived in or near Burlington and came for the day. Relatives and others visiting from afar might stay for a week or longer, and were often put to work helping with various camp tasks. Popular recreation options for guests included fishing, hiking, swimming, and venturing down the hill for day trips to Lake Champlain, local barn auctions, and ice cream socials in nearby Waterbury.

Edie Wurm Jensen recalled, "We never felt we had to 'entertain' guests. Although there was always plenty of food, people usually made their own breakfasts. Lunch was typically soup and sandwiches... My mother would heat up a whole lot of canned soup, put it in a big tureen on the table, put out loaves of bread with lots of sandwich makings. I think everyone who came knew this was mountain time with just barely enough modern amenities to live comfortably." Generous suppers were made "from scratch" using local vegetables and meats purchased from the Jonesville store.

Also keen to enjoy the fruit of the land, Dr. and Mrs. Wurm cultivated a vegetable garden, as well as large patches of blueberries, raspberries, and rhubarb. The small apple orchard they planted along the driveway included Macintosh, Cortland, and Northern Spy trees.

When World War II ended in 1945, so too did the danger which inspired Honey Hollow Camp. Nevertheless, the Wurms continued to visit their cherished mountain escape for another 20+ years, making many improvements to the property and cabin, as well as erecting additional purpose-built structures to round out the grand compound.

Summer, 1942

Dr. Wurm's Jeep at the Jonesville Store, 1953

First-ever family meal inside the cabin—atop sawhorses, 1941.

Dr. Wurm grills fish in the fireplace, 1948.

Supper indoors with the Wurm, Samson & Holmes families, 1941.

Lenora Wurm (Carl's Mother), Julie Arcuni & Edith Wurm, 1948.

Edie Wurm's 11th birthday party, July 1948.

Summer lunch outdoors with the Holmes & Samsons, 1942.

Dr. Wurm, Edie Wurm and Dr. Samson, 1941.

Photos: John A. Wooden

Dr. Wurm and taxidermied hunting trophies, c. 1944.

THE SPORTSMAN

As a bachelor in his 20s, Dr. Wurm took several big game hunting trips to Quebec and British Columbia, where he shot the moose, grizzly bear, caribou, mountain goat and other taxidermy trophies which would later define the cabin's interior decor. During most of his Honey Hollow years however, his medical practice kept him busy making house calls in New York during hunting seasons; he managed just a handful of Vermont deer hunting trips, but in 1949 began hosting an annual week-long fishing trip for a group of city friends and relatives. During the Wurm family's annual July visit, he often enjoyed fly-fishing Preston Brook's crystal clear waters for their elusive and delicious "brookies" (brook trout), as well as hunting the occasional wild rabbit.

Dr. Wurm fly-fishing on Preston Brook, Summer 1942.   A single day's catch of brookies, Summer 1942.

LOGGING CAMPS

By the late 1940s, Honey Hollow's sawmills were gone. Limited logging operations continued however, most notably at a camp owned by the Burt Lumber Company, photographed here by Carl Wurm in 1948. Located just 200 yards from the Wurm's northern property line where the old Farnsworth mill once operated on Preston Brook, the camp served as a base of operations, and consisted of simple shacks to shelter horses and house loggers on site. By this time bulldozers routinely supplemented horses for skidding felled trees from deep in the forest to Honey Hollow Road, where they were loaded onto huge logging trucks for transport to the Plant & Griffith lumber mill in nearby Jonesville.

Edith & Edie Wurm visiting logging camp, Summer 1948.

Aproned woman greets logger, Summer 1948.

A team of horses pulls out Dr. Wurm's snowed-in Cadillac, Winter 1942.

WHITE CHRISTMASES

Each year the Wurms would return to Honey Hollow for Christmas vacation, usually joined by the Samsons and Holmeses, and remain through New Years. Not wishing to brave pre-Interstate winter roads, the Wurms typically boarded a Pullman sleeper train at Grand Central Station in Manhattan on the evening New York City schools let out, arriving refreshed in snowy Vermont the next day. Either the Samsons or Holmes would taxi them to the base of Honey Hollow, where everyone would bundle up for the final leg of their journey: an open-air horse-drawn sleigh ride up the steep, snowy road courtesy of the Derosias or Leo Lafreniere.

While Honey Hollow winters are harsh, the Wurms and their guests enjoyed the modern cabin's creature comforts. Its diesel generator not only kept lights twinkling on a freshly cut wild Christmas spruce, but also powered the electric pump that made winter indoor running water possible, thanks to Professor Holmes's ingenious lower dam on Homestead Brook. With no central furnace, the cabin was kept cozy with not one, but three concurrent roaring wood fires: one in the big central fireplace, one in a top-loading Ashley stove just ten feet from the hearth, and the third in a twin Ashley located in the cellar, situated to warm the floors and prevent basement pipes from freezing.

The group enjoyed magical Vermont holidays, replete with roast goose, Wurm & Holmes' famous eggnog, and the ceremonial burning of giant hardwood yule logs. Days brought boundless outdoor fun including sledding on steel-railed Flexible Flyers, skiing, and skating and ice fishing atop the frozen pond.

Keeping warm by the fire. From left: Dr. George Samson, Edith Wurm, Edie Wurm & Mabel Samson, Winter 1942.

First winter vacation in Honey Hollow, 1941.

Plowing the driveway, 1943

Homestead Brook lower dam winter water supply, 1942.

Ice skating on the pond, 1944.

Ralph Maynard Holmes

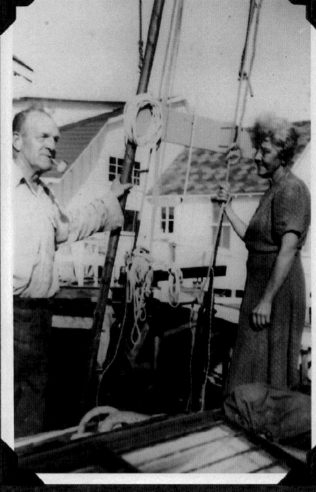

Ralph & Mary Holmes aboard "Electron II"

PROFESSOR RALPH HOLMES - THE ENGINEER

Ralph Maynard Holmes was a central and indispensable figure in the development and history of Honey Hollow Camp. He and his wife Mary were close friends of Carl Wurm's in-laws, Dr. George Samson and Mabel Samson, and were involved early in the search for property on Dr. Wurm's behalf.

A physics professor and Chair of the University of Vermont Physics Department, Ralph was a skilled engineer with a passion for building and boats. The Holmeses were childless, and Ralph gave generously of his free time to the Honey Hollow Camp project, including designing the gravity-fed water system and diesel generator "power plant" that made the Wurm's rustic camp the valley's first "modern" structure with running water and electricity.

Once the cabin was completed, Ralph and Mary became its de facto off-season "innkeepers" while the Wurms were in New York City, visiting most weekends and vacations from autumn through spring. Summers were devoted to the Holmes' other great love: their 40-foot yawl "Electron II" on the coast of Maine, where Ralph generated extra income adjusting nautical compasses aboard private boats.

More than a caretaker, Ralph was an active partner and driving force in the property's evolution. His many contributions spawned a warm and productive friendship with Dr. Wurm which lasted the remainder of their lives. Ralph Holmes died July 28, 1967, aged 80. Today, Edie Wurm Jensen credits Professor Holmes' involvement in the project as transformative, making the property vastly more refined and livable than it would have been been otherwise.

Holmes at site of Homestead Brook upper water supply.

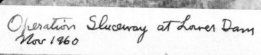
Operation Sluceway at Lower Dam Nov 1960

Holmes' Homestead Brook "winter water" lower dam.

Holmes' subterranean "power plant" generator room.

Sunday Apr 10.
Warm weather, the syphon does not take care of the inflowing water. It is running over the top of the dam. Water pump just into operation.

Holmes' pump maintaining pond water level.

Holmes enjoying his pipe at the camp fireplace.

Holmes felling pine tree for woodshed rafters.

An early letter from Professor Holmes to Dr. Wurm, penned shortly before final closing on the Old Farm property.

HONEY HOLLOW
CORRESPONDENCE
OCT. 6, 1941 1948

THE UNIVERSITY OF VERMONT
BURLINGTON, VERMONT

DEPARTMENT OF PHYSICS

January 12, 1941.

Dear Carl:

I have the honor to submit the following report on a trip made to H. H. P. Estates on January 9, 1941:

Arrived at the LaFrenier house at 2:35 P.M. Decided to leave the car there and to walk up to The Estates. Walking up found that the road was plowed wide enough for a car and that there would have been no difficulty in driving up with chains. Air temperature at La Frenier's was 30° F.

Walking up the road we (Mr Rooney, Instructor in Physics, went with me) soon caught up with Mr LaFrenier, who, as we afterward discovered from the NO TRESPASSING signs is superintendent of the Estates. Taking care to inform Mr LaFrenier that were were visiting the property on business we walked along with Mr LaFrenier and just astern of his pair of horses engaged in hauling an empty sled up the road for logging purposes. Mr LaFrenier and his team turned to the left before we reached the line of H.H.P. We arrived at the north line of H.H.P. at 3:07 and there found a very pretentious NO TRESPASSING sign. Mr La Frenier had already informed us that he had that day persuaded two hunters not to hunt on the lands of H.H.P. Arriving at Perilous Brook we noted a good flow of water under the ice. Mr Rooney, who is an experienced planter of trout fry and a former president of the Chittenden County Fish and Game Club informed me that Perilous Brook is very suitable for the planting of trout fry. At 3:17 we arrived at another NO TRESPASSING sign on the right side of the road and near the ruin of Jewett's Barn. We found still another sign just north of the entrance to the proposed location of the house.

We observed the flow of water in the small brook which runs about 150 ft north of the proposed location of the house and I estimated it as 6 pails per minute. Probably the flow in Perilous Brook is three times this amount.

We found about 1ft of snow on the cleared land near the house location. We observed that some work had been done towards removing the remains of the house from the cellar. Mr LaFrenier had told us that he and a small crew had spent one afternoon at this but that winter conditions were such that he concluded it better to wait for warmer weather before continuing this work.

We set up a sighting compass on the cellar wall at the N.W. corner and found that the direction of the wall (the west wall) is 11° east of magnetic north which means that it is 4°.5 west of true north. It seems possible that this house was intended to be about North and South when is was built. The enclosed map shows the angles. We then measured the walls of the main house and of the ell.

Possibly Polaris was sighted on

To obtain a rough idea of the typography we sighted in the directions N, NE, E, SE, S, SW, W, and NW from the N.W. corner of the wall and estimated the elevation of the ground relative to the top of the wall at distances of 50' and 100' from the N.W. corner of the wall. You will see for example from the map that at 50' north from the wall we estimated the ground to be 25' below the level of the wall. You will notice that the ground in the immediate vicinity of the wall is in all places below the level of the wall except that at 100' from the corner in a S.W. direction the ground and the wall are at the same level. We used a carpenter's level to aid us in these estimates.

On the map I have indicated the approximate locations of the sun at sunrise and at sunset on June 21, September 21 and December 21. I have made allowance for the fact that the mountains will hide the sun for a time after sunrise and for a longer time just before sunset.

Mr Rooney considered the view from the house to be excellent. The air temperature at the house was 26.° F.

We did not go to the remains of the Haunted House as it was getting a little dark.

We returned to our car and on the way back we met the boys who live at the end of the road returning from school. After consuming a quart of hot coffee and several cookies we got under way for Burlington, arriving home at 5:30.

In the belief that the formal part of my letter is ended, I now join with Mary in wishing you and Edith a very happy new year.

In hoc,

Ralph

Holmes (center, leaning in vest & cap) directs water flow measurement at Homestead Brook (Honey Hollow Stream).

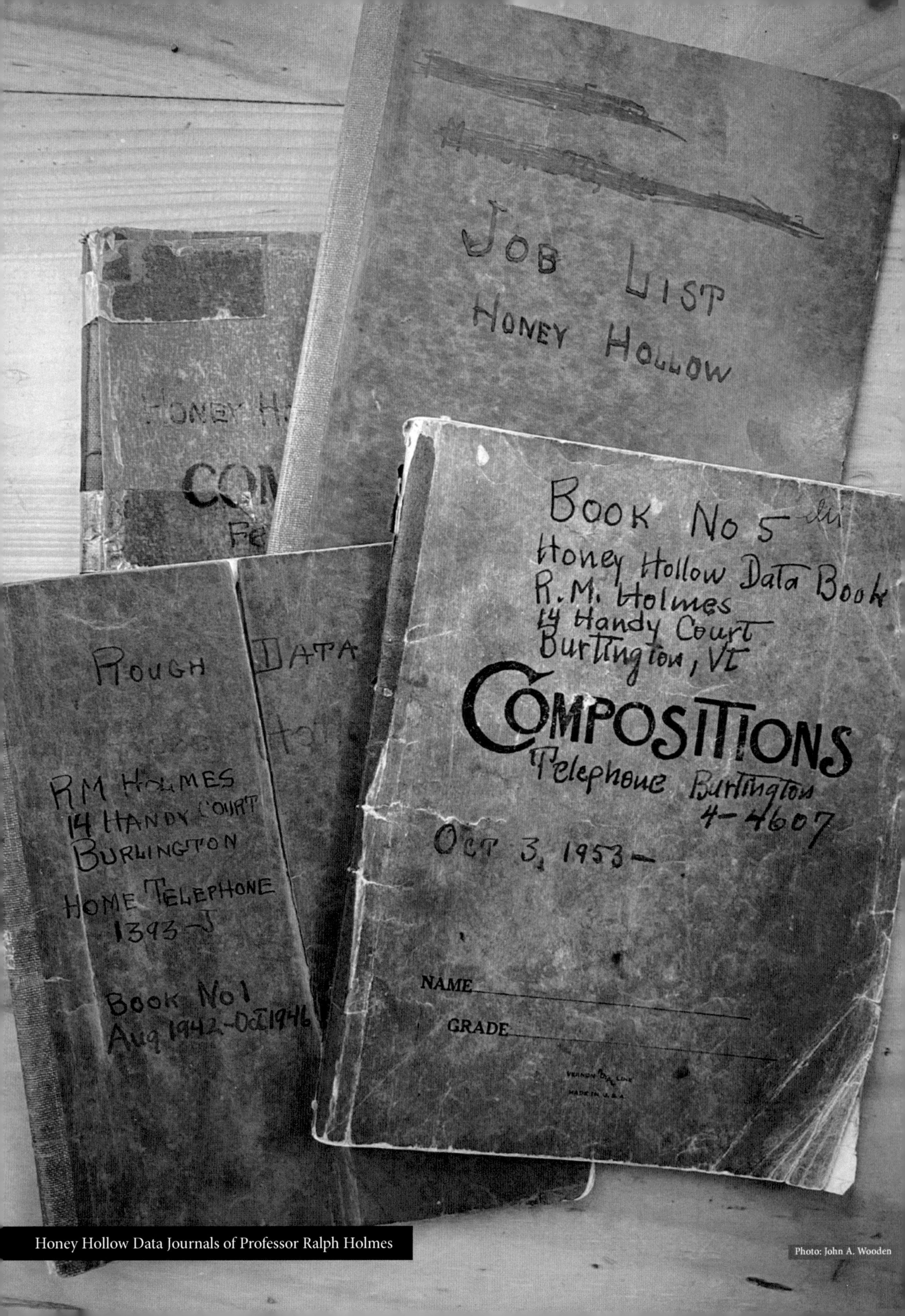
JOB LIST
HONEY HOLLOW
Book No 5
Honey Hollow Data Book
R.M. Holmes
14 Handy Court
Burlington, Vt
COMPOSITIONS
Telephone Burlington
4-4607
Oct 3, 1953 -
NAME
GRADE
ROUGH
DATA
RM HOLMES
14 HANDY COURT
BURLINGTON
HOME TELEPHONE
1393-J
Book No1
Aug 1942 - Oct 1946

Honey Hollow Data Journals of Professor Ralph Holmes

Photo: John A. Wooden

Holmes' Subterranean Power Plant, 2007

A PEN PAL PARTNERSHIP

"Skipper" Holmes kept "Doc" Wurm up to date on off-season happenings in Honey Hollow via a steady stream of letters and photos sent via US Mail. Of their 18-year correspondence, fewer than two years worth of Holmes' letters (totaling almost 100 pages!) survived among Dr. Wurm's papers. With their playful banter and Dr. Wurm's hand-written margin notes for his responses, the missives paint a lively, intimate portrait of the warm friendship between the two men, and their shared boundless passion for every detail—no matter how small—of living life to its fullest in Honey Hollow.

HONEY HOLLOW
CORRESPONDENCE
OCT. 6, 1946

Continuing to answer your letter, I do not see how the cow could have gotten into the raspberry patch unless the gate was opened and she was turned loose therein. I have never seen the cow without a chain. She goes away unless she is chained. And, with a chain she could not have gotten as far into the patch as I saw the manure.

Oct. 11, 1949

At one time I was interested in bees and still think it would be fine to have a few hives at H. H. I think a good hive of bees will furnish about 60 lbs of honey. (I have just called up Rooney who had a few hives at his place and he says this is about right if the bees are attended to. And, honey is worth 50¢ per pound.)

Nov. 23, 1948

(also, I like it)

Wednesday afternoon we had a hail storm. The hail stones were about as large as beans but quite round. We put out two pans and collected enough to have hail stone cocktails before dinner.

Nov. 18, 1948

There was a lot of excitement at Derosias Sunday. Carleton was going inside old Jim's stall to lead him to water. I expect old Jim was startled in some way. Roger thought Carleton may have fallen down in old Jim's stall. The horse kicked Carleton. Beverly was in the barn. She ran to the house; Roger came to the barn; got mad with old Jim; started to give the horse a whipping and was in turn kicked by the horse. The injuries were: Carleton with a broken forearm and some minor bruises; Roger with a minor scalp wound and a minor leg injury which made him limp all day but which is not serious. Roger took Carleton and Leo to the Mary Fletcher Hospital in Burlington.

Oct. 14, 1948

When we arrived at the cabin on Sat., Jan 15 the minimum thermometer registered -7; the cabin was at 25; the cellar, 34 and the vault, 39. On Jan. 22 the minimum was 3; cabin, 31; cellar, 34 and vault 37.

Jan. 24, 1949

Remembering the shipping you sent about gum drops for baiting mouse traps, we are now using them. One day I saw a mouse in the living room; baited a trap with a gum drop and in 3 minutes heard it snap. Got the mouse.

Aug. 29, 1949

use worms at night

I tried fly fishing one night by the light of the full moon. The trout were not interested.

Oct. 21, 1948

I talked with Lafreniere about transportation up the hill. At present he has one old horse which is completely out of commission and which he plans to shoot soon. His other horse is so wild and nervous that even Lafreniere cannot use him. He will soon get rid of this horse. He will sometime get other horses. He has only the forward bob-sled of a pair of bob-sleds.

Oct. 11, 1949

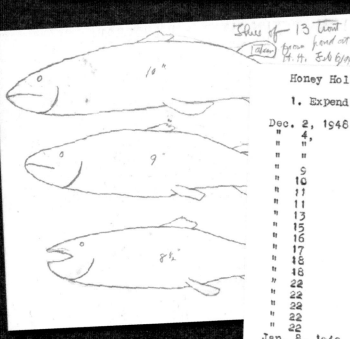

Three of 13 trout taken from pond at H. H. Feb 6/1949

10"

9"

8½"

Honey Hollow Operating Fund.

1. Expenditures.

Date		Description	Amount
Dec. 2, 1948.		Excess expenditures as by report.	$ 5.92
"	4,	Gasoline for plant	4.90
"	"	Pipe threading compound	.35
"	"	Everett for labor	2.50
"	9	Spark plugs	1.29
"	10	Liquor for Christmas	56.85
"	11	Bolts	1.80
"	11	Everett for labor	5.00
"	13	Snow fence and steel posts	17.50
"	15	Winter oil for plant motor	2.89
"	16	Machine work	.50
"	17	T. A. Haigh Lmbr Co for Homasote	8.78
"	18	Plumbing supplies	1.42
"	18	Everett for labor	6.00
"	22	Hardware	1.05
"	22	Gasoline for plant	6.25
"	22	Food for Christmas vacation	62.69
"	22	Chain saw rivets	.48
"	22	Plant & Griffith for lumber	8.26
Jan. 8, 1949.		D. Larned. Your bill for cigarettes, mittens, gloves, films, etc.	19.72.
		Total	$214.15

Jan. 13, 1949

We should be planning our Christmas season and should move to the cabin all of the non-perishable articles we can while we can drive up there. What do you want for liquor for Christmas or will we join Alcoholics Anonymous?

As ever,

Ralph

The usual. Will send check later, but too much here now.

Nov. 1948

THE WOODSHED

When temperatures dropped that first fall and winter of 1941, the Wurms quickly discovered that keeping warm in their new cabin was no small feat; its high elevation meant deep snowfalls and bone-chilling winds swirling down from Camel's Hump, which quickly sapped away any accumulated indoor warmth. And while they'd outfitted the cabin with more than ample means of heating, the enormous fireplace and two Ashley stoves had voracious appetites for wood. To keep the fires burning, logs had to be fetched from the frigid outdoors all throughout their days and nights at camp. After the second winter, plans were hatched to erect a grand woodshed just steps from the back door. Professor Holmes tackled the project with gusto, not only designing the shed, but also felling trees for beams, axe-cutting them, and constructing most of the building himself.

Ralph Holmes strips pine bark from beams, 1944.

Woodshed footings and initial framing, 1944.

The wood shed should go along faster now. It was slow work putting on the rafters. I had to do a lot of hunting in the old lumber pile to find suitable stock and had to hew both ends of each rafter to set these ends in mortises in the plates.
Best wishes,

Ralph

Oct. 4, 1944

Holmes atop woodshed frame.

Holmes shovels snow off roof.

Nailing up exterior boards.

90

Actually keeping the shed filled with firewood proved another matter however, and many of Holmes and Wurm's letters touched on the pressing theme of "woodin'". Recurring quintessentially Vermont topics included how much wood supply remained, who was cutting more wood (or neglecting to cut it), and from where and whom they might source their next loads of firewood.

> Now, coming to the fire wood situation. No wood has been put into the shed since you were at H. H. last summer. I expect it is less than half full. I think there is no more short wood than we will want to burn during the Christmas season.
>
> Oct. 14, 1948

> The present condition of the wood shed is: There will be enough wood for Christmas, but, no more. If Leo stays away, Everett and I may cut up the maples and may increase the supply.
>
> Dec. 2, 1948

> Very little wood this week end. Less than 1/2 cord on Saturday afternoon and the boys were both away all day today. I have next Friday and Sat. off. Everett has promised to work on wood.
>
> Feb. 20, 1949

Several years later, always seeking new ways to streamline the cutting and stockpiling of wood, Holmes proposed adding a "saw house" to the shed's north end. The enclosed extension, completed in 1950, featured a trap door for sweeping out dust from the large power saw housed therein, and became a kind of workshop headquarters for Holmes' many projects.

Framing of saw house extension.

Saw house extension nears completion.

> If we have a wood sawing machine, I hope that it can be just north of the present wood shed and that we can have enough space to keep the stove wood under the same roof as houses the saw. The wood we will saw will be kept near the cabin and another location for the saw would require so much more handling of wood. Today I looked over the ground just north of the present wood shed and concluded that it would be O. K. for an extension.
>
> Feb. 10, 1949

POTATO FARMING

Amidst severe food shortages in 1942, President Roosevelt used his radio "fireside chats" to encourage Americans to help the war effort however possible. Staples like potatoes, a then-common Vermont crop, were in particularly high demand. And so in the spirit of patriotic duty, Dr. Wurm purchased a horse-drawn potato digger for $185, and entered into a revenue-sharing contract with his tenant Leo Derosia to plant, tend, harvest and market potatoes. Derosia, occupying the old farmhouse with his family of six, enlisted his sons and horses to plant a 15-acre crop. So promising was their debut in the spring of 1943, Dr. Wurm renewed Derosia's contract for another year. The 1943 crop delivered its anticipated profit, but despite a strong start in 1944, Derosia's struggles with alcohol resulted in much the second year's crop being left to rot in the ground. Disappointed, Dr. Wurm scuttled the short-lived farming venture, marking the end of commercial agriculture in Honey Hollow.

Honey Hollow

Green Mountain Potatoes

Grown by

OPEN VALLEY FARM, BOLTON, VERMONT

Address correspondence to

GEORGE D. SAMSON
266 MAIN ST., BURLINGTON, VERMONT

Leo is digging potatoes and the crop is coming out very well. He has sold $1100. worth of potatoes and has many more to dig. He said that the piece of potatoes southeast of the cabin paid all of his expenses with $200 left over. He talks of planting a larger acreage next year and he also said that he plans to plow up a lot of the field and seed it down for hay. (I remember you told me that you had suggested this to him) He is getting $2.25 per hundred pounds in bags at the Demo house and without grading. That is these potatoes are the "run of the field". He has graded only a very few;he gets a larger price for these.

Excerpt of letter from Professor Holmes to Dr. Wurm, October 4, 1944.

Leo & Carlton Derosia harvesting potatoes.

View northeast of Honey Hollow potato field in bloom.

CERTIFICATE OF POTATO SEED INSPECTION

VERMONT DEPARTMENT OF AGRICULTURE

This Certificate is issued on the

THIS IS TO CERTIFY that the

Dr. George D. Samson   Burlin

Name of Grower   Post O

has been inspected by the duly authorized agent of the Vermont Dep

July 13, 1943

(1st Inspection)

and the following conditions were noted:

Variety   Green Mountain

DISEASES OR IMPERFECTIONS	PER CENT	
	1st	2nd
Mosaic	Trace	.4 of 1
Leaf Roll	1.2	.4 of 1
Fussrium Wilt	-	-
Early Blight	-	-
Late Blight	-	-
Rhizoctonia	Trace	Trace
Tip Burn	-	-
Blackleg	-	-
Insect Damage	-	-
Missing Hills	-	-
Weak Hills	-	-
Yellow Dwarf	-	-
Spindle Tuber	-	-
Varietal Mixture	-	-
Giant Hill	-	-

T

ment

in the

scribed

No. 10

AG-1

AGREEMENT BETWEEN DR. CARL WURM AND LEO DEROSIA IN A POTATO
RAISING PROJECT FOR 1942 IN HONEY HOLLOW, BOLTON, VT.
※※※※※※※※※※※※※※※※※※※※※※※※※※※※※※※※※※※※※※※

Leo Derosia is to furnish all labor, horses, and his
equipment and farm tools necessary for the proper planting,
growing, and harvesting a crop of potatoes on as much land as he
can thoroughly care for; and do what trucking is necessary in
connection with getting the crop under way and marketing it.

He will store the potatoes in a place mutually agreed
upon, care for them after storing, and properly grade and pack
them for market. If bags or other containers are needed for
marketing the potatoes, their cost will be financed by Dr. Wurm
and be included in the general expense.

Dr. Wurm is to furnish the land, and finance without
any interest charge, the purchase of seed potatoes, fertilizer,
spray material and insecticides; rental of planter or any other
machinery or material to be agreed upon as necessary for the
proper growing of the best crop of potatoes possible, subject to
the advice or recommendation of the County Agent.

The above mentioned expense shall be divided, after
marketing the potatoes, on a 50-50 basis, and the resulting
profit, if any, shall be divided, -- Sixty (60) percent to
Leo Derosia, and Forty (40) per cent to Dr. Wurm.

Carl Wurm Jr,
by George D. Samson
Leo Derosia

Bolton Vermont,
April 27, 1942.

MARSH-ALLEN CO.

THE FARM EQUIPMENT SERVICE STATION
BARRE, VERMONT

Telephone 140

Y

Sold to *Dr. Carl D. Wurm Jr. Bolton Vt.*

Sp. 13 -

1 - potato digger - $85.00

Paid. M. E. Allen.

April 17, 1943.

cover season of 1943 on same terms

Carl Wurm Jr.
by George D. Samson
Leo Derosia

THE "SWIMMING POOL"

Inspired by his parents' home in Pleasantville, New York, Dr. Wurm decided to mark Honey Hollow's first post-war summer in 1946 by building a "swimming pool" 100 yards south of the cabin. There, the large field formerly planted with potatoes was naturally bisected by a wet depression caused by bubbling ground springs and a small, unnamed stream flowing northeast towards Preston Brook during the spring runoff season.

Taking advantage of these natural water sources, a bulldozer was brought in to carve out the area, depositing the dirt in an earthen dam to create a ten-foot deep hole. Professor Holmes designed a system for drainage, and augmented the water supply with an irrigation pipe to reroute additional water from Homestead Brook. Within a few weeks, the new pond was full, a dock was erected, and the summer fun ensued, replete with floats and boats and splashing children.

Each summer the Wurms hosted competitive swim meets at the pond, and Dr. Wurm and Professor Holmes enjoyed considerable success stocking it with minnows and trout for their own fishing enjoyment. During winter vacations, snow was shoveled off the frozen pond to create a large skating rink.

As the years and decades have passed, the man-made pond has become home to many native species including red-spotted newts, four-toed salamanders, bullfrogs, American toads and turtles. Mallard ducks are frequent visitors, beavers have made multiple (thwarted) attempts to build dams, and today the pond continues to be a popular watering hole for deer, moose and black bears.

Edie Wurm & Derosia kids swimming.

Building the dock. From left, Dr. Wurm, Roger Derosia, Edie Wurm, Anne Imhoff, Everett & Leo Derosia.

Clearing stones from bulldozed area.

The new pond with Camel's Hump in background.

THE "NEW BARN"

After the Old Farm's two large barns and back buildings were dismantled in 1941, little storage space remained in the surviving granary, or "corn barn". With the Derosia family's livestock occupying that structure, it became clear within a few years that another building was needed to store the various mowers and other equipment required to properly maintain the large property.

In the fall of 1947, construction began on a three-level "new barn" immediately adjacent the granary, on the spot where the Old Farm's large southern barn once stood. Carved into the hillside, the new barn's bottom level was outfitted with four stalls for the Derosia's horses and two cows. The center, road-level floor was used for parking cars and storing equipment. The top level was a working loft, complete with a chute for dropping hay to the animals two stories below, and quickly became a favorite play spot for young Edie Wurm and her friends.

Surviving letters from Professor Holmes indicate that at one point following the demolition of the old farmhouse in 1950, Dr. Wurm entertained converting the new barn's upper levels into an apartment for a caretaker or guests, but he was advised the structure was not suitable. This was in part because while little expense had been spared to build the cabin, the new barn was erected on a budget. Its exterior of white asbestos shingles tacked to a green lumber frame made for a compromised aesthetic charm, but more significantly, its foundation of inexpensive cinder block proved no match for the annual ravages of winter ground frost cycles, resulting in extensive structural damage over the years. Ultimately not destined to stand the test of time, the "new barn" was demolished in 2009.

Ice skaters with "new barn" foundation, Winter 1947.

Old farmhouse, granary and new barn, Winter 1948.

New barn after razing of granary & farm house, Winter 1951.

New barn undergoing foundation repair, Spring 1952.

Photo: Gary Bressor / U.S. National Register of Historic Places

New barn, Summer 1993.

Photo: Gary Bressor / U.S. National Register of Historic Places

Cabin and new barn, Autumn 1993.

The "New Barn" enters its final winter, November 2008.

"THE ANNEX"

The small extension on the cabin's northwest corner was first conceived as a bay window to brighten the living room and provide a better view of approaching vehicles. As the Wurms discussed it more, the scope of the project increased into a sunny little room they later dubbed "The Annex". It was erected in the spring of 1953 mostly by Skip and Mary Holmes, atop a foundation built by Ronnie Lafreniere and Robert Cote. The original west wall window was re-installed and joined by two others, including a plate glass "picture window" facing Bolton Valley. The Annex became a popular place to read and chat, and during summers served as a greenhouse for Mrs. Wurm's beloved African violets.

Bushey is nailing boards on the roof as fast as Skip can cut them to proper length and bevel.

Ralph Holmes Photo Caption

Annex under construction with Professor Holmes cutting roof boards in foreground, Spring 1951.

Edith Wurm's African violets inside the Annex, 1963.

Edith Wurm making applesauce outside the Annex, 1963.

103

Sunset on Bolton Valley beyond "The Annex", Autumn 2016

Photo: John A. Wooden

THE 16mm COLOR REELS

While color photography, and color home movies in particular, were beyond the reach of most Americans during the 1940s, the Wurms were fortunate to possess an early Kodak 16mm motion camera, which they used to capture moments during their visits to Honey Hollow from 1944-1948. The images spanning these pages are single frames captured from 20 minutes of surviving motion pictures, which can be viewed, as narrated by Edie Wurm Jensen, at honeyhollow.net.

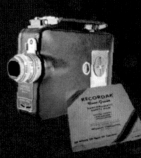

Holmes & Wurm carry in the yule log.

Fetching firewood from the woodshed.

Edith & Carl Wurm, Summer 1963.

New stone wall flower garden, built 1963.

TWILIGHT OF THE WURM YEARS

By the 1960s, Carl was winding down his medical practice in New York, freeing the Wurms to pass more time enjoying Honey Hollow—and each other. In 1961, they doubled their summer stay to two months, then in 1962, extended it further to spend five full months in Vermont, remaining until late October to enjoy the stunning fall foliage. Edith's days were filled with swimming, canning blueberries by the score, visiting friends, making watermelon pickle, and tending to her "Garden of EDE-n". Carl worked the land, clearing brush and cutting grass with his shiny red Simplicity ride-on mower. The summer and fall of 1965 were to be the Wurms' last time together in Honey Hollow. Carl died of heart complications at 74 on May 5, 1966. After his death, Edith continued to visit Vermont during the summers for many years, staying mostly on Lake Champlain. She passed in 1993, aged 93.

Carl Wurm haying with Jeep, Summer 1963.

Edith Wurm haying, Summer 1963.

Edith Wurm at the "Garden of EDE-n", Summer 1963.

Dr. Wurm: "My New Cadillac", Summer 1963.

Mrs. Wurm in the Annex, Ashley stove in foreground, Autumn 1964.

Hunting Party with Dr. Wurm at right, Autumn 1965.

Atop Camel's Hump Summit, Summer 1971. From left, Edie Wurm Jensen, Martha Wooden,
Rosemary Wooden, Jenni Jensen, Jennifer Wooden, Grace Wooden & Kenneth Wooden.

ENTER THE WOODENS

In 1970, four years after Carl Wurm's passing, his grown daughter Edie Wurm Jensen was living in South Carolina. That March, her involvement in the League of Women Voters led her to attend a "How to Change the System" education conference in Washington D.C. There, she happened to meet a young teacher from Pennsylvania named Ken Wooden. They sparked up a friendly conversation, during which Edie mentioned the remote Vermont camp which had been willed to her. When Ken expressed interest, she graciously and spontaneously invited him, his wife Martha, and their three daughters to visit Honey Hollow. Never one to pass up an invitation, Wooden followed up soon after.

The Woodens made their first trip to Vermont in July of 1970, and like Carl Wurm 30 years prior, were instantly enchanted. A warm friendship blossomed between the two families, and soon the Woodens became Honey Hollow regulars. Living over a thousand miles away, Edie was grateful for trusted friends who could visit Vermont more often than anyone else in the extended Wurm/Jensen family, lest the unused cabin fall into a state of neglect.

But by 1974, the burden of remote ownership of the high maintenance property weighed on Edie. The Wurm estate was subdivided into three parcels: 355 acres were sold via the Nature Conservancy to the State of Vermont for inclusion in Camel's Hump State Park, 235 acres were held in Trust, and the remaining 53 acres, including Honey Hollow Camp, were sold to Kenneth & Martha Wooden.

In 2021, Edie reflected of the sale, "Where would I have found someone other than Martha and Ken who shared my deep love of the cabin, the valley, the mountains—Honey Hollow!?"

Honey Hollow Camp, July 1970.

Martha, Jennifer, Ken, Rosemary & Grace Wooden, July 1970.

Friends of Ours

Name	Address	Date

August 1, 1970 Thanks for the best vacation we've ever had. Its the first time we're not ready to go home. You rolled out your most beautiful weather! The Woodens will never forget Honey Hollow

Ken, Martha, Grace
Rosemary & Jennifer
Bucks Co. Penna.

Guest book entry from the Woodens' first visit to Honey Hollow.

Martha, Grace & Jennifer Wooden, July 1970.

Ken Wooden, July 1970.

The Woodens: Ken, Martha, Grace, Rosemary, Jennifer and John, Christmas 1974.

Rosemary, Jennifer, Grace & John Wooden, Summer 1973

Jennifer, Rosemary, John & Grace Wooden, Summer 1975

Ken Wooden with Leo & Judy (Preston) Lafreniere, October 1972.

A GUARDIANSHIP

On May 16, 1975, the Kenneth & Martha Wooden Family took legal possession of this beautiful & sublime tapestry of nature within the Valley of Honey Hollow, Vermont. We, as those before us, will never own this property. It is ageless and defies ownership. The wisdom of nature, the view, the movement of night, are owned by no one and nature must smile on mortals who think they do.

For as long as this land is in the legal possession of Kenneth & Martha Wooden and their children, Grace, Rosemary, Jennifer, John Allen and their offspring, we as a Family will be vigilant & act as guardians of this tract. If you come to desecrate, you only destroy a portion of yourself and not that which future seasons guarantee. If you come in Peace, then you, too, shall share the Spirit which the great mystery of life has endowed within this Land.

Go softly good People . . .

The Wooden Family — 1980

"The old Lakota was wise. He knew that man's heart away from nature becomes hard; he knew that lack of respect for growing, living things soon led to lack of respect for humans, too. So he kept his youth close to its softening influence."

Chief Luther Standing Bear

The Wooden Family 2021—Clockwise from left: Scott Webb, Rosemary Wooden Webb, Preston Webb, Carl Mitchell, Ward Wooden, Anna Liza Bella, Chase Mitchell, Simone Wooden, Grant Mitchell, Jennifer Wooden Mitchell, Sophia Webb, John A. Wooden, Sarah Gilbert, Calvin Gilbert, Grace Wooden Gilbert-Davis, Ken Wooden, Martha Wooden

A MOUNTAIN LEGACY

For nearly 50 years, Ken and Martha Wooden, along with their four children's families including eight grandchildren, have devoted themselves to preserving the historic legacy of Honey Hollow Camp. In 1994, the 53-acre property was expanded to 72.5 with the purchase of an adjoining parcel to the east: the old Jennings/Allen homestead along the banks of Preston Brook. The Wurm's cabin has been renovated to include a traditional standing seam metal roof, and expanded with an architecturally faithful post-and-beam eastern addition, which includes windows salvaged from the early 19th century Honey Hollow school house. The surrounding clearing has been slowly enlarged to reclaim portions of the Old Farm's once-sprawling meadows, and the 60 acres of forested land placed in a long-term Vermont Forestry Management Plan dedicated to preserving the health of the woodland ecosystem and its habitats of native fish, wildlife, and plants.

Ken Wooden has long used the affectionate euphemism "polishing the jewel" to refer to the hard work required to maintain this unique and beautiful property. He credits this labor of love as the key to long life, fulfillment and spiritual contentment. Whether by nature or nurture, his progeny have taken this credo to heart, practicing a family philosophy rooted in a love of nature that guides their mission to ensure this magical place is preserved for generations to come.

Martha Wooden,

Ken Wooden, 2019

Photos: John A. Wooden

Honey Hollow viewed from western ridge, 2021

2020

BIBLIOGRAPHY

Personal Papers of Dr. Carl Wurm, Jr. - Estate of Carl Wurm, Jr.

Prof. Ralph M. Holmes Personal Correspondence to Carl Wurm, Jr. (1941-1949)

"Honey Hollow Data Books" - Prof. Ralph M. Holmes (1942-1954)

Edie Wurm Jensen
- Interviews by John A. Wooden via Zoom Videoconference (Feb. 2021-Apr. 2021)
- Email & Postal Correspondence to John A. Wooden: (May 2020-May 2021)

Leo Lafreniere
- Interview by Ken Wooden & Gary Bressor - 8mm Video Tape (Aug. 3, 1993)

Edith Samson Wurm
- Interview by Ken Wooden - VHS Video Tape, (September, 1987)

Bolton Vermont Town Clerk - Property Deeds & Town Records

National Register of Historic Places Registration Form: Prepared by Gary Bressor with Ann Cousins and Chris Fichtel (1993)

"Art Notes: Exhibition Looks Back at Local Architect" by Nicola Smith, Valley News: Part of the Newspapers of New England Family - vnews.com (April 13, 2016)